OFF MY CHEST

Tales of a Cardiothoracic Surgeon

KEYVAN MOGHISSI

First published in Great Britain 2018

ISBN 978-1-9996143-0-0

A CIP record for this book is available from the British Library.

Cover by: Sirpa Pajunen-Moghissi
Typeset by: Marten Sealby

CONTENTS

CONTENTS

FOREWORD

This is a selection of stories, based on my diaries and case-notes, stretching back over a long career in cardiothoracic surgery.

Essentially, they are all true stories. But I've changed the names to protect the innocent – and myself!

As I write this, I've just celebrated my 90th birthday. I'm still in good health, I'm glad to say, and continue to be engaged in Medicine.

I'd like to thank my long-time colleague and friend, Kate Dixon, who witnessed some of the events described herein, and whose assistance was invaluable in reading, re-reading, and proofing this selection. I'm also grateful to my daughter-in-law, the artist Sirpa Pajunen-Moghissi, for the cover design, and to my new-found friend, Jonathan Gems, who helped me whip the stories into shape.

Most of all, I'd like to thank my wife, Alex, who has put up with me all these years and, without whom, nothing would have been possible.

Professor K. Moghissi

1

DAGGER IN THE HEART

In September 1970 I started work at Castle Hill Hospital, near Hull, in Yorkshire, as its only consultant in cardiothoracic surgery.

When I arrived, I found a devoted staff and plenty of good will, but there were no intensive care nurses, the surgical equipment was out-of-date, and the condition of the theatre, and the wards, was appalling.

After getting things cleaned up, I organised an emergency team that could be ready, in 40 minutes, to open the chest and carry out major operations.

At that time, the routine for emergency admissions was for all cases to go to Accident & Emergency at Hull Royal Infirmary, before being transferred to a specialized unit.

My hospital was five miles away so, if the emergency required cardiothoracic surgery, treatment was delayed by at least two hours.

In time, I was able to persuade the authorities to send these cases directly to me.

On Thursday the 24th of December, 1970, soon after setting up the emergency unit, I was looking forward to Christmas Day.

This was to be my first Christmas as a consultant and, according to tradition, I was to cut the turkey and, with the help of the ward sister, dish out the Christmas lunch. This was a great privilege!

On that particular Thursday, I was doing my rounds of the wards, when I received a call from Bridlington Hospital, which was about twenty miles away.

"Are you Mr M, the new thoracic surgeon?"

My caller was the consultant orthopaedic surgeon at the Casualty Department. He sounded alarmed.

"I have a man – a police inspector. He's got a number of stab wounds. And a kind of dagger. It's still in his chest. I think it's pierced his heart. What shall I do?"

I asked him to send the man, who was receiving blood transfusions, directly to our operating theatre, and emphasized that no attempt should be made to remove the dagger.

Hastily, I arranged for a radiographer to be on hand, and prepared for an emergency operation.

The patient arrived in a pool of blood, and was taken to be X-rayed.

At that time, I had one of the best anaesthetists I've ever known, named Stuart. When confronted by emergencies, Stuart was as nerveless as a stone.

After Stuart had put the police inspector to sleep, I surveyed the man's injuries and documented his skin lesions with my camera.

There were nine wounds of different depths, each with a diameter of between 2 and 4 centimetres. There was a knife, like a dagger, up to its hilt in his chest. The X-ray confirmed that the instrument had gone through both his lung and his heart.

The left lung had collapsed and there was a large volume of blood and air in the left chest cavity.

Drainage of the chest was the first priority, which I dealt with in the anaesthetic room, extracting a good litre of blood and lots of air bubbles, which indicated laceration of the lung.

Then the patient was wheeled into the operating theatre.

I'd dealt with stab wounds before, but mostly in hospitals with better facilities than we had at Castle Hill. But there was no point in thinking about the equipment we didn't have. So, I formulated a plan of action, and explained it to the operating team.

"Our aim is to remove the dagger, and repair the heart as quickly as possible, with a minimum of bleeding and – God willing – with the heart still beating."

Once everyone, including the additional nurses I'd brought in, understood their roles, we got started.

The chest was opened by cutting through the breastbone (sternum), leaving the dagger in place until everything was ready for repair.

With a great gush of blood, the knife was removed. No worries though! I lifted the heart with my left hand and, working within the pool of blood, used my right hand to close the wounds of the heart with a series of stitches.

This was done in less than a minute.

Then I turned my attention to the lung.

We completed the repair of the lung, and the wounds of the interior chest wall, and controlled the bleeding.

Finally, the main operation was over – and we were pleased because the heart was still beating.

But there was more to do. The chambers of the heart were lacking blood, and the patient's blood pressure was low.

We began a series of blood transfusions.

Suddenly his heart stopped.

I immediately began cardiac massage, by squeezing and releasing the heart muscle, and the patient was ventilated with 100% oxygen.

As I massaged the heart, I asked Stuart to check the equipment, including the gas cylinders and anaesthetic machine gauges. Everything checked out fine.

But something was wrong. I had to think fast. My patient was dying.

"The problem is there but you're not seeing it," I said to myself. "It's there but you're not seeing it!"

A small thought flickered from far away.

"Stuart?" I looked at the anaesthetist, as I was putting my back and shoulders into the cardiac massage. "Have you checked the patient's temperature?"

"No, I haven't, but I will."

He did this and reported a reading of 28C.[1]

"Dear God!"

The heart could not beat when the temperature was that low! This was due to a large, and rapid, transfusion of cold blood. What we needed was warm saline solution to put into the chest and around the heart.

[1] 82 Fahrenheit.

I said to the charge nurse: "Do we have a warm cabinet in the theatre?"

Her reply was 'yes,' but it could only heat 3-4 pints of fluid. Not enough for the amount of saline we needed.

"Okay." I turned to the nursing sister, Dorothy. "Can you give me bowls of warm water from the hot water tap, cooled with cold water to a temperature of 45 degrees?"

"Are you sure, sir?"

"Yes, sister!"

We poured many litres of warm water into the left chest and around the heart, and sucked it out again – a kind of warm water irrigation – as I continued to massage the heart.

At 35-36 degrees, the heart began to beat, like an old-time locomotive that starts by puffing before slowly picking up steam.

Finally, the heart was beating strongly, and we had superb blood pressure.

I put my hands together and waited, crossing and re-crossing my fingers, until I judged we were safe to insert the chest drains and close the sternal wounds.

An hour later, the man woke up from the anaesthetic. My patient was saved, and it was almost Christmas.

Perhaps one interpretation of the star of Bethlehem story might be what happened when the thought appeared – like a new star in the night sky – that the heart was too cold.

Is this fanciful? No doubt. But I definitely felt something 'other' had intervened.

Sister Dorothy, who'd been testing the temperature of the water, and passing bowls of warm water to us around the table, later spread a story that, while I was waiting with my hands clasped together, I was praying.

I wasn't praying. At least, I don't think I was. But, I might have been. All I know is, I was somewhere else.

On Christmas day, the police inspector was sitting up in bed, tired but well, and asking for something to eat. The answer was 'not yet' – not until I'd performed my special 'consultants-only' privilege of carving the turkey.

Later that day, I learned that our patient was not – as we'd all assumed – a victim of attempted murder, but a failed attempt at suicide.

The police inspector's recovery was gratifyingly rapid and, by early January, he was ready to go home. But I was worried about him. He was so withdrawn and depressed, I was afraid he might try to take his life again.

I suggested he see a psychiatrist. He thought it a good idea but, as I was leaving, said: "Could I have half an hour of your time?"

"Of course. Would this evening be all right?"

That evening I went to his room.

He was looking extremely miserable. He grabbed my hands and said: "My hands tried to end my life. Your hands saved it."

I had a flashback of the blood jetting towards me, after I'd removed the knife.

Then the unhappy police inspector told me about the many overwhelming pressures in his life.

We talked and talked and, finally, his mood began to lift.

By the time I left, he was saying his greatest worry was that he'd ruined his wife and daughter's Christmas.

"Make it up to them in the new year," I said.

"I will." He said. "I will. That's a promise."

He was discharged from the hospital, and his superiors had no objection to him continuing his job as a high-ranking police officer.

Several months passed and, one afternoon, as I was driving through Bridlington, a police car appeared behind me, flashing its lights. My first thought was I was speeding but, when I stopped the car and looked round, I recognised my dagger-in-the-heart police inspector.

As I wound down the car window, he approached, smiling and waving. He wanted me to have a cup of tea with him at the police station. How could I refuse?

At the station, he introduced me to his colleagues, saying: "If you ever have a chest injury, or are assisting in one, make sure you call this man!"

As it happened, many years later, after the police inspector had retired, I needed his advice about a young patient who, as the result of a drunken brawl, had been arrested.

He agreed to help the boy by appearing in court as a character reference. I'll never forget him in the witness box.

Speaking directly to the judge he said: "Sometimes people make a mistake but, if they're helped, they can change and never make that mistake again. This happened to me."

The judge nodded, and there was something about his nod that told me the boy would be given a second chance.

And he was.

2

CHEST DEFORMITIES

There are many types of chest deformities, but they generally fall into two groups:

1) The front of the chest and sternum are concave in the middle: a 'sunken' or 'funnel chest,' known as *pectus excavatum.*
2) The sternum is convex, or bowed outwards: a 'pigeon chest,' known as *pectus carinatum.*

As a surgical registrar at the Victoria Hospital in Blackpool, I learned to perform standard chest operations. But it wasn't until 1961, when I became a senior surgical registrar at Southampton Chest Hospital, that I became fascinated by the chest wall's architecture, and its relation to respiratory function.

After two and half years of research, I won a Wessex Hospital Board's *Research Essay Competition* for my work on the subject.

By 1970, when I started at Castle Hill, I'd carried out over 300 operations on patients with chest deformities – most of them done for cosmetic reasons.

In the 1980s, I had scores of patients with chest deformities on my waiting list. This was despite me being very selective in offering reconstructive surgery.

My long waiting list was because the operation was 'cosmetic,' and cancer, or cardiac cases, had priority. Another reason was that most thoracic surgeons wouldn't do cosmetic operations on the NHS. They'd only do them privately.

For myself, I did cosmetic cases whenever I could, such as when I had a cancellation, or when I was on call over the weekend. This was possible in the old days, when consultants were in charge of running their departments.

(Things changed after Margaret Thatcher's government monetized the National Health Service and managers came in to run the NHS as a business, rather than a public service.)

I usually gave children priority because a chest deformity can adversely affect the spine as the child grows up. My next priority was young women, whose social lives were sabotaged by their misshapen chests.

These young women would frequently change boyfriends, or avoided socializing altogether. A few were engaged, but waiting for an operation before getting married, because they were embarrassed about 'undoing the bra.'

Rachel was an attractive 23-year-old who, were it not for her chest deformity, could well have been a beauty queen.

Rachel's dream was to wear a bikini, go to the beach, and have a boyfriend.

Having endured a year on the waiting list, she'd decided to contact my secretary to ask if she could be treated privately.

I arranged for her to come in to discuss her reasons for not wanting to wait another 3-4 months.

She turned up with her mother.

"I'm desperate," she said.

"She truly is," said her mother. "I never hear the end of it."

For the past year, I've been saving up for a holiday," Rachel said.

"She has," confirmed her mother.

"But I'd rather spend the money on having the operation done privately."

That's right," said her mother. "As soon as you can manage it – if that's all right."

In those days, I carried out private operations on Saturdays, when my specialized assistants were available, and I'd just been told we'd had a cancellation.

"Rachel," I said, after a pause. "How would you like to have your operation next Saturday?"

"That soon?"

"Yes."

She asked how much it would cost.

"Nothing. It'll be done on the NHS."

"How can you do that?" she asked.

"Easy. We've had a cancellation. And, all being well, you can stay in the private room, which is vacant this weekend."

"Are you sure?"

"Absolutely."

Her mouth fell open, and she looked at her mother. Then she looked back at me, her eyes welling with tears.

"I don't know what to say."

"Then don't say anything."

I arranged to have clinical photographs taken to document the pre-operative picture of the deformity for comparison with pictures after the surgery. Other pre-operative preparations were also organized.

She was admitted on Friday and, on Saturday, I carried out the operation.

The result was excellent. I'd managed to make the incision small and the scar invisible, unless the breasts were lifted up. She now had a fantastic chest to go with her good looks.

A month later, I saw her at Outpatients. She asked if she could go on holiday.

"Of course, you can!"

Two months later, I received the following letter:

Dear Mr. Moghissi,

Hello, I am writing to thank you for making a wish come true for me. It has just hit me that I no longer need to worry about my funny-shaped chest as it is not funny shaped anymore!

Last week my mum booked our holiday – a couple of weeks in the Isle of Wight. I went out and bought a swimming costume (one that didn't come up to my neck!) and a bikini. So, all those eligible young bachelors had better run for cover!"

All my love,

Rachel x

3

BEFORE DYING

George Boulanger, the twentieth century Romanian violinist and composer, gave the title *Avant de Mourir*[2] to a piece of gypsy music he wrote that was fashionable in the 1950s.

Having played the piece in my youth, I think both the music and title fit the following story:

Early in 1988, a man in his late thirties was sent to me with a terminal case of cancer of the oesophagus.[3] He couldn't take anything by mouth and, when he tried to drink, he would cough so badly that he'd almost lose consciousness.

Not only was the cancer very advanced, but it had spread to some of the intra-abdominal organs, and entered the trachea.[4]

Martin (that was his name) had completed a course of radiotherapy that, while relieving his difficulty in swallowing, had caused a fistula[5] to form between the oesophagus and trachea.

[2] Before Dying.
[3] The gullet, connecting the mouth to the stomach.
[4] Windpipe.
[5] A small, abnormal tunnel connecting two internal organs.

Due to the tumour blocking the oesophagus – and the fistula above this obstruction – whatever he took by mouth went straight through his windpipe into his lungs

The challenge was to provide a way for Martin to receive nutrition, and reduce the suffering caused by the passing of saliva into his trachea.

After doing extensive tests, I employed bronchoscopy [6] and oesophagoscopy [7] to visually inspect the trachea and oesophagus. During this inspection, I also cleaned his bronchial tubes of food debris.

Next, I used a laser to remove the tumour.

Then, to allow him to breathe more easily, I discussed carrying out a tracheotomy [8] with him and his partner – a very nice Australian lady named Julia.

Thanks to these procedures (and drugs to suppress his coughing attacks), he was able to drink, and swallow soft food, without distress.

The patient and his girlfriend, Julia, were troubadours who travelled Europe, earning their living by singing and

[6] Looking into the airways through a viewing instrument called a bronchoscope.
[7] An endoscope for inspecting the interior of the oesophagus.
[8] An opening is made in the windpipe (trachea) and a tube inserted, to allow air into the lungs.

playing to small audiences. They loved this nomadic, gypsy-like lifestyle. However, Martin had always kept a nest in Yorkshire, which they'd moved into after he became ill.

We needed to make arrangements for Martin's continuing care.

His nearest relative was a niece who'd shown no interest in her uncle until he'd fallen sick. According to Martin, it was his small property that had stimulated his niece's new-found feelings of kinship.

It was obvious to everyone at the hospital that Julia was the person closest to Martin. She was utterly devoted to him.

Sadly, after a week or so, it became clear that, despite all our efforts, Martin would end his life at the hospital.

One day, Julia gave me a note from him, asking me to see him.

When I saw him, I thought he was going to ask me for help with the pain. But it wasn't that. It was something quite different.

His partner (and love of his life) had no legal right to any of his possessions – not even his body after his death. As an Australian, she was in the UK on a restricted visa. Martin was distraught at the prospect of her being forced to leave the UK.

"But what can I do about this?" I asked.

Due to the tracheotomy, Martin couldn't speak, so he wrote on a piece of paper.

'We want to get married.'

"Married?" I said, in astonishment.

'Yes. Please can you talk to Julia?'

'How can I arrange a marriage?' I thought. 'It's impossible.'

The next morning, at breakfast, I felt a faint glimmer of hope. During my time as a consultant at Castle Hill, I'd become acquainted with several clergymen of different denominations. Two years before, I'd even given a talk at a multi-denominational church conference.

My first port of call was the hospital chaplain. He dismissed the idea out of hand. A wedding couldn't be done, he said, because Martin wasn't a church-goer and hadn't been baptised.

I must say I considered his attitude rather deplorable. Still, I knew a Catholic priest – famous in Hull – who was always willing to lend a helping hand, so I left him a message to call me.

He called that same evening.

"Hello Father," I said.

"This is official, isn't it?"

"How did you know?"

"Because you called me Father."

I laughed. "You're right!" Then I explained the situation.

He suggested I call a certain Protestant clergyman who, as luck would have it, I knew – having recently helped a couple of his parishioners.

Sadly, his response was negative. To perform a marriage at such short notice was out of the question.

"No one would do this."

"No one?" I said. "Are you sure? How about Jesus? If Jesus were here, would He do it?"

The vicar fell silent.

After a long pause, he sighed and said: "All right. I'll do it."

"Thank you."

"Where?"

"In the hospital."

"In the *hospital?*"

"Yes."

"Are you serious?"

"Yes."

There was another long pause.

"*Where* in the hospital?"

"In the side ward."

We fixed a date for five days hence.

Regrettably, Martin's condition worsened, and his breathing became so laboured that we had to move him to

Intensive Care to be ventilated. He needed to be alive, and fully conscious, for the wedding.

The marriage of Martin and Julia was performed by this wonderful Protestant vicar in the presence of an officer of the civil registry, myself, my registrar, and some of the nursing staff.

Martin died peacefully the next day.

4

A WINTER NIGHT IN SCARBOROUGH

It had been a long, hard, but good day and, for once, it looked like I was going to get home before 11 pm.

"I'm getting out of here," I told my registrar.

"I think I'll stay and study."

My registrar, David, was sitting the second and most difficult part of his Fellowship examination (FRCS)[9] in a few weeks' time.

"Are you going home, boss?" he asked.

"Yes, I have a date with a French lady, a descendent of an Italian called Stradivarius."

"You lost me, boss!"

I explained that Antonio Stradivari was a great 17th century luthier – a maker of string instruments – whose violins have a unique tonality, and a price tag of £40-50 million. I obviously don't have a Stradivarius but I do have a 19th century French copy, which I named 'Madame Antonia,'

[9] Fellowship of the Royal College of Surgeons.

and which I cuddle under my chin whenever I get the chance.

I was about to leave the office, when the phone rang. I thought it was my wife but it wasn't. It was Tony – a delightful doctor in his early forties, from Scarborough – a seaside town 40 miles from my centre near Hull.

Once a week, I visited Scarborough Hospital to consult at their outpatients' clinic.

"I apologise for calling so late," said Tony, "but I've got a very sick patient here with a high temperature and a collapsed lung."

The patient was a local dignitary named Lord Bufton who needed immediate attention but, because he'd lost a family member at another North Yorkshire hospital, refused be treated at Scarborough.

He wanted Tony to prescribe him some medication so he could go down to London to see a surgeon who was his personal friend.

This friend was Sir Thomas Holmes Sellors, one of the UK's pioneers of cardiothoracic surgery, and a former president of the Royal College of Surgeons.

Tony had called Sir Thomas who told him there was no need for Bufton to go to London because "One of my best assistants is in Hull who is perfectly capable of doing anything I could do."

Hence the call.

Sir Thomas had been one of my mentors, and a man I greatly admired so, naturally, I felt obliged to see the patient.

I phoned Alex, my wife, and told her the bad news. Would she mind making me a snack? Then I'd be off to Scarborough.

When I arrived home, Alex was oddly nervous. Usually, she was fine with me being called out on emergencies but, this time, she wanted to come along.

So, we took a blanket, and a thermos of tea, got in the car, and set off.

Normally, I enjoy driving along the narrow, winding roads of North Yorkshire but, this time, it was different. It was a very cold night. There was no moon, no street lighting, and animals kept skipping out in front of the car.

To avoid a fox (my wife said it was a wildcat), I almost put the car in a ditch.

When we arrived at the hospital, it was after midnight. We got out of the car, and hurried through the freezing darkness to the barely-lit main entrance.

I hadn't noticed the door before because, every time I'd been there, the door had been open. It was a strange door, ornamented with medieval shields and spikes.

My wife, Alex, suggested we might have come to the wrong address.

"I think this is Bluebeard's Castle," she said.

Next to the hospital's intimidating door, was a circular brass bell with a button in the middle of it. I had to press the brass button three times before we heard footsteps. Then the door opened, revealing a gaunt hospital porter, with a pronounced stoop.

A somnolent night nurse led me to the first floor – the private ward – which was a row of cubicles, each with its own washbasin and commode. Tony was standing next to a bed occupied by a plump, late-middle-aged man with grey, flyaway hair.

The man was flushed, breathing rapidly, and pushing the bed sheets away with his legs.

This was Lord Bufton.

"So," he spluttered. "You're the man Tom says is as good as he is."

"Sir Thomas is very generous."

I asked him questions about his illness; then I made a clinical examination, including auscultation[10] of the chest.

There was little doubt that Lord Bufton's right chest was filled with fluid – probably pus. I also suspected a lung abscess. He'd had a chest X-ray, so I went to the sister's office,

[10] Listening to the internal sounds of the body, usually using a stethoscope.

and studied it on a viewing box.

It confirmed my provisional diagnosis of empyema.[11]

But I needed one more test.

I told Tony I was going to carry out a chest aspiration.[12] This would not only confirm the diagnosis, but reveal what needed to be done.

I then informed Lord Bufton I was going to anaesthetise the skin, then aspirate his chest to get a sample of fluid. I asked him to sit up.

He huffed and puffed but couldn't do it.

Eventually, with the help of a strong sister, we got him sitting up.

"Ooh!" he gasped. "All right, doctor, I suppose if you insist on doing this, I shall have to go along with it."

I cleaned the skin on the back of his chest.

"What do you expect to find?"

I pretended not to hear him, so he repeated his question as I quickly aspirated half a 50ml syringe of smelly pus.

I showed him the syringe.

"*This* is what I expected to find."

[11] Purulent collection in the chest/pleural space.

[12] A small needle or tube is inserted into the space between the lung and chest wall to remove fluid that has accumulated around the lung.

The pus was thick and offensive, and I was sure there wasn't just one pool of it, but several small ones, separated by walls of fibrous tissue.

The pus had to be evacuated via an operation. Insertion of a single tube couldn't drain it all.

I discussed my plan with Tony in his office. He agreed, and we went to speak to the patient.

"Well sir," I said. "I now have the diagnosis."

"And what is it?"

"In simple terms, your chest is full of pus. This needs to be evacuated urgently, and the chest cleaned out, so the lung can expand. It will require an operation."

"When do you propose to operate?"

"Now."

"You mean – tonight?"

"I mean now."

"Have I any choice?"

"Not if you intend to live."

"What are my chances?"

"Provided this has not resulted from a malignant condition, there's a good chance of a complete recovery."

"You seem very confident."

"I'm confident enough to say, sir, that were I in your place, I wouldn't hesitate."

"I see. Well, you seem to know what you're doing so, go ahead. Do your worst."

We took him into the theatre.

Unusually for a physician, Tony changed into surgical attire, and came in to watch the procedure and assist me.

I made a small skin incision and opened the chest. I cleared the debris and pus, closed the wound, and the patient was transferred to his room.

We took an X-ray, which showed that the lung had already expanded.

When I came downstairs, I thought my poor wife must be frozen in the car, but then remembered I'd asked the ghoulish porter to look after her.

I found her in the consultant's room, resting but awake. The porter had made her a cup of tea and brought her a digestive biscuit.

"They look after you really well here, don't they?" she said.

Lord Bufton's recovery was without complications. But he demanded to be discharged from the hospital 3 days after the operation. This was highly irregular, but I agreed because he had 24-hour nursing cover at his stately home. And I arranged to see him twice a week for three weeks.

Lord Bufton's country seat was not far from my route

to Scarborough, so it was no great inconvenience to make a short detour to go and see him.

I visited him five times in all and, on every occasion, I admired the furniture, paintings, objects d'art, and especially the grand piano in his drawing room.

His bedroom had an ensuite bathroom with an antique toilet. I noticed the toilet each time I went in there to wash my hands. The name 'Thomas Crapper & Company' was inscribed on the cistern and the ceramic bowl.

This name Crapper was not unknown to me. In fact, before moving to Yorkshire, I'd made a point of learning as much about the county as I could, which included learning about Thomas Crapper, who was born in Thorne, Yorkshire.

I bought a small book about him entitled, '*Flushed with Pride,*' by Wallace Rayburn, and it has been in our downstairs toilet for many years.

Some of our guests, including visitors from abroad, seem to stay an unusual length of time in the downstairs toilet, compared to the upstairs one.

This is based on an 'observational study' however, and not the result of a clinical trial!

5

NICOLA

Nicola's birth was greeted with rapture by her parents, who had been counting the days to see their new baby's face.

At the maternity unit, the midwife spotted a problem with the baby's swallowing. Saliva was flowing from her mouth. There was a blockage in her throat.

Oesophageal atresia[13] was suspected and the baby was rushed to my cardiothoracic centre.

It's hard for the parents of a healthy baby to conceive of the anxiety experienced by parents whose baby has a birth defect. Sitting in a hospital room, waiting for the doctor to come with test results, is agonizing.

It's stressful for the doctor too. Personally, I've always found these situations daunting. The doctor needs to be compassionate and understanding but, at the same time, have an unclouded mind in order to develop a clear and decisive plan of action. He must rise above the stress, so as not to jeopardize sound judgement and good performance.

[13] Oesophageal atresia is a defect that affects the alimentary tract. The oesophagus ends in a blind-ended pouch rather than connecting to the stomach.

The belief that doctors are trained not to be emotionally involved – or get used to this sort of thing – is poppycock. The distress of a mother who's been told her baby needs a risky operation, is enough to keep any surgeon up all night.

My personal therapy for stress is to retire to my office for 20 minutes and listen to the music of Johan Sebastian Bach. Why Bach? Why is his music so effective?

The only way I can explain it is that there's something in the structural complexity and contrapuntal warmth of Bach's music that both listens and responds. The music listens to, and responds to, laments.

I think God listens, but he doesn't respond – at least not to me, and not audibly.

Little Nicola *did* have oesophageal atresia, together with some other congenital abnormalities, so I was worried. When you open the chest of a baby with birth defects, it can be like opening Pandora's Box – you never know what other problems you may find.

But, in this case, none of the other problems were life-threatening and, happily, her anatomy was favourable to a straightforward reconstruction of the oesophagus.

The operation wasn't difficult and, when it was done, I told her parents I expected a speedy recovery. And, sure enough, it wasn't long before she was able to take fluids by mouth.

After she was discharged, Nicola came regularly to my outpatients' clinic, and I watched her grow from a baby into an exceptionally affectionate little girl.

Accompanied by her mother, she would enter the consulting room, walk to my desk, stretch up on her toes, put her arms around my neck, and kiss me on the cheek.

Then she'd show me her latest drawings.

"I did this one for you!" she'd say, with a big smile, and present me with one of her drawings.

By the time she was 10, I had enough of her pictures to mount an exhibition!

One morning, she gave me a drawing of her dog, which I thought exceptional. She'd really caught the dog's character. I still have it, in a frame, in my office at the Yorkshire Laser Centre.

I've often wondered how sick children, like Nicola, are able to endure so much hardship. Many of them are also touchingly understanding of their parents, and the others who take care of them.

I'm also impressed, and humbled, by some of the parents, whose stoicism and devotion can be extraordinary. Interestingly, I've heard quite a few of these parents say that caring for their disabled child brings them a unique kind of happiness.

As Nicola grew up, I researched how to deal with her other deformities, which were increasingly affecting her quality of life. I felt sure a solution could be found, and was hopeful that developments in bio-plastics would soon provide materials able to remedy the defects in her chest-wall.

But, as time passed, she became very short of breath. In spite of this, every time I saw her in the clinic, and asked how she felt, she'd respond with a big smile.

"I feel fine!" she'd say.

I used to wonder how this smiling child was getting on with her parents, and how things were at home. Were the smiles and sweet behaviour only for my benefit?

The answer came from a letter I received, much later, from her mother.

"Nicola was a lovely baby and developed into a lovely child, having an exceptionally wonderful nature and personality. She attended primary, junior and senior schools as a normal child.

Due to her weak chest, she was prone to chest infections, which was the cause of most of her problems and discomfort. Despite all her problems, and slight of build, she hardly had any time off school at all.

Also, despite all her problems, handicaps and suffering, she never complained and always seemed happy. She did very well at school. She obtained 8 GCSEs and left school at 17. She was very good at art and loved doing it.

She loved animals and her biggest love was horse riding. She went to a local stables where she got tremendous enjoyment riding her favourite pony, Dapple. She also had a dog, of which she was exceptionally fond.

All through her life she was fortunate to have a wonderful set of girl friends who looked after her.

She got on very well with her brother James, who was 6 years younger, who was always a big help to her.

After leaving school, she obtained work at a friend's care home. At the age of 17 she had the misfortune of contracting measles, which attacked her heart from which she subsequently died.

'We still miss our daughter so much that we talk about her often, as does the whole family.'

I can still see little Nicola entering my clinic, and I celebrate her courage and her lovely nature, by looking at her drawings.

I was raised in a religious Bahá'í[14] family, and the love of God has been planted in my soul. However, when I'm lost in sorrow, I look up and ask God: "Where are you?"

Comfort comes not from prayer but from listening to J. S. Bach's 'La Chaconne.'

[14] Bahá'í teaches the worth of all religions, and the equality of all people.

6

THE MAN WHO DEFIED DEATH

In the 1950s, when I was a medical student in Geneva, we were taught to treat patients and their families with humility and tact. If the patient had a serious disease, and wanted to know the truth, he should be told the truth. If he *didn't* want to know, he should not have the information forced upon him.

And we were told never to play God by telling a patient how long he or she had to live.

When asked "How long have I got?" common practice is now to give a time-frame, such as: 'six to nine months,' or 'two to three years.'

This was forbidden when I was a student, and whenever I hear a patient say: "The doctor told me I've got three months to live," I gnash my teeth.

It's bad practice because it's dishonest (no-one can ever know how long you have to live), and because of its psychological impact.

Psychological causes can have physiological effects.

We know this because when we're embarrassed, we blush – a physiological effect. When sad, our eyes produce tears – another physiological effect. Words have consequences – *especially* when they come from your doctor.

In 1976, I was reminded that, even when every indicator says death is imminent, you can never be sure.

This case concerned a man who'd had part of his windpipe removed for cancer, followed by reconstructive surgery and a patch graft.

In the early 1970's, surgeons were working to produce a material suitable for grafting major airways, such as the trachea (windpipe), and the two main bronchi that conduct air to the lungs. One of the materials thought suitable for this was a synthetic mesh of polypropylene – called *Marlex Mesh* – which was produced as a sheet.

Unfortunately, the use of this mesh was often attended by failure because it was porous. When implanted, it allowed air to leak out, which could lead to infection, and a breakdown of the suture line.

It occurred to me that the air leak problem might be solved if the mesh were covered with a sheet of biological material – such as the pericardium (the membrane which envelops the heart.)

After 2-3 years' work, I demonstrated the viability of

this idea, and was experienced enough to be able to select suitable cases for treatment. Furthermore, by employing this pericardium membrane, I could take on the more difficult cases.

One of these difficult cases was Mr Tuohy, who had cancer growing in the upper part of his right lung, and also in the lower part of his trachea.

Rather than removing the entire lung, which would have badly affected this 62-year-old's quality of life, I decided to excise the tumour, along with the upper part of the right lung, together with a small portion of the lower trachea.

After that, I reconstructed the airway by putting my composite material over the defect as a patch graft.

The operation went well, and Mr Tuohy seemed to be on the mend. Then, a few days later, he was blitzed by septicaemia, abscesses in the lungs, and purulent discharges from the wound and drain sites.

The whole team went to work on him with cardiac support, ventilatory assistance, and antibiotics.

This improved his condition, but something was wrong. He wasn't responding properly.

Then, all of a sudden, his heart and lungs failed.

Quick action by the nursing staff saved his life, but he was left barely conscious, with symptoms of extreme shock.

I assembled my colleagues for an emergency consultation. The situation was critical. Based on multiple indicators, our patient was at death's door. Everyone agreed he couldn't last the night.

Up until then, every patient I'd treated with the new graft had done well – and we had copious clinical and X-ray evidence that all the grafts had been accepted. One patient, who died later in an accident, had a post mortem that gave good proof of this. Microscopic examination had shown complete incorporation of the graft within the host tissue.

So, why had this one failed?

I was utterly confounded. There was no sign of the graft separating from the host tissue but, in the presence of such massive infection, there was no way it could possibly hold.

I met with the family, who were gathered in the ward, and told them of the gravity of the situation. They were tearful, but grateful for the struggle we were making to help their father.

At about 2 am, after further efforts, I accepted defeat, and summoned the family again to tell them the bad news.

I was plagued with guilt. A serious deficiency in a surgeon is not knowing your own limitations – something I always warned my assistants against. Had I been too ambitious? Should I have judged Mr Tuohy inoperable? If I'd judged him inoperable, he might have had a few more months with his family.

How do you tell the family that their loved one is dying? Despite my long experience, I still find this dreadfully hard to do. Also, I needed to know if the graft had failed and, if so, why? There was only one way to do this: an autopsy. But I couldn't ask the family for permission to do an autopsy. It would be far too insensitive. This delicate matter would be best addressed after the patient had passed away.

"Courage, mon brave!" I told myself, as I entered the Sisters' office, where the family was waiting.

The wife, the son, and the daughter were sitting there. Three pairs of anxious, tearful eyes. Both children were grown up, and in their 30s. I'd seen them before individually, but never all three together.

I sat down.

"I'm sorry to say that it's not looking good..."

Before I could finish, the daughter said: "Is Dad going to die?"

"I don't know. But I think he'll need a miracle to get out of this."

"What went wrong?" asked Mrs Tuohy.

I told her it was most likely a failure of the graft.

She looked at me. "You're terribly tired," she said.

Dear God, I thought, what a wonderful lady to think of me at a time like this!

Then she asked if I were religious.

"As a matter of fact, I am, yes. But I don't go to a church or a temple."

"Well you see, I believe in God," she said, "and, if it is His will, I will have to accept it."

I nodded.

They asked if they should go home. I said they were welcome to stay if they wanted to. It was up to them.

After a quick look at her grown-up children, Mrs Tuohy said: "I think we'll go home and come back in the morning."

"Fine."

"What happens when, you know, when he…passes away? Will he have a post mortem?"

"That depends. But let's talk about it when the time comes."

To my surprise, she said: "I want you to know we have no objection to a post mortem – if you can learn something from it." Then she added: "Do I have to sign anything?"

"Yes. But don't worry about it now. If the time comes, we'll let you have all the information."

"If I go now, I don't want to come back," she said. "I'll leave that to my son. Can I sign the form now?"

So, it was agreed.

I gave her the information, and she signed the form.

As they left, the daughter asked: "Is there anything more you can do?"

I shook my head. "I don't think so. But we'll keep trying."

"Is there anything *we* can do?"

I thought for a moment.

"Yes. You can pray."

***

Against all the odds – and to the amazement of my team – Mr Tuohy survived. The graft did not fail, after all.

When we were sure he was out of danger, I sat down to rest and saw myself back in the classroom in Geneva, with our bushy-bearded Professor of Medicine saying:

"C'est Dieu qui decide du moment où l'esprit quitte le corps et pas le médecin." [15]

Mr Tuohy recovered, was discharged and, according to my follow up records, lived for at least another eight years.

[15] "God decides when the spirit leaves the body - not the doctor."

7

THE APPLE TREE

It was a Saturday afternoon in mid-August, and I'd gone to the hospital to catch up on some research work.

I was sitting on the floor of my office, surrounded by piles of case-records, when there was a knock on the door.

I wasn't expecting anyone, and the only people who knew I was there were the doctor on duty, the sister in Intensive Care, and the telephone operator.

At that time, I had an Italian Research Fellow and, guessing it was him, thought I'd show off my Italian.

"Avanti!" I sang out. "Avanti!"

But I'd locked the door from inside, which rather spoiled everything.

I hurried over to open it.

But it wasn't my assistant. It was the Senior House Officer, Dr Ramesh, and his wife – both very red in the face.

Before the door was fully ajar, they rushed in, almost tripped over my case-notes, and began shouting and waving their arms about.

"We were nearly arrested!" cried Dr Ramesh, his neck

veins bulging.

"A nurse called him stupid!" cried Mrs Ramesh.

"This is outrageous!" raged Dr. Ramesh. "Utterly and totally outrageous!"

"I thought you were off duty this weekend," I said.

But they carried on shouting and gesticulating.

"Please! Please calm down!" I pulled out two chairs. "Both of you. Sit down – please – and tell me what happened."

Still complaining, they sat down.

"We had an argument," panted Dr. Ramesh.

"With one of the nurses," snorted Mrs Ramesh.

"From the medical ward."

"We told them he was a doctor!" protested Mrs Ramesh.

"She called the police!" declared Dr. Ramesh, incredulous.

"She accused us of stealing!" yelled Mrs Ramesh, boiling with fury.

"Please calm down!"

"But, sir," said Dr. Ramesh, "We had to convince them! We had to convince them I was a doctor!"

"You must do something!" demanded Mrs Ramesh. "This is unacceptable!"

"They wouldn't let us go!" complained Dr. Ramesh.

"Who wouldn't let you go?" I asked.

"The police!" screeched Mrs Ramesh.

"They wouldn't let us go until I convinced them I was a doctor in your department!" spluttered Dr. Ramesh.

"You must do something!" insisted Mrs Ramesh.

"Why were you in the medical ward? Were you seeing a patient?"

"No," said Dr. Ramesh. "It didn't concern the work."

"What did it concern?"

"She accused us of stealing apples!" wailed Mrs Ramesh.

"What did it concern?" I repeated.

"Well sir, I was up an apple tree..."

"This cannot be tolerated!"

"What were you doing up an apple tree?"

"Taking a picture."

"Taking a picture?" I asked, in amazement.

"Yes."

"A picture of apples?"

"No, a panoramic view of the hospital."

Light dawned, and I almost burst out laughing.

Dr. Ramesh, a keen amateur photographer, had wanted to shoot the hospital from a high vantage point. There were no tall buildings at the hospital, so – as his wife watched from below – he'd climbed an apple tree.

A nurse in the medical ward, saw this through the window, thought he was stealing apples, and called the police.

This had infuriated Dr. Ramesh and his wife, who then called the nurse 'ignorant,' and 'an idiot,' and told her to mind her own business, and 'go away and clean some bed pans'!

In those days, a call from a hospital nurse prompted a rapid response from the police. They were there within minutes.

But they soon saw it was all a misunderstanding, and left.

Ramesh and his wife had a huge dust-up with the nurse, and insisted on an apology. But the nurse demanded an apology from Dr. Ramesh for calling her a 'scrubber'!

I asked the doctor, whom I valued as a competent member of our team, to write a report on the incident, and then I went to find the Matron.

Thanks mainly to the Matron's diplomatic actions, both parties received their apologies. But she tore a strip off the nurse for leaving her patients, and told Dr. Ramesh – in no uncertain terms – that, under no circumstances, was he allowed to insult the nurses!

8

MY FRIEND KALMAN

Kalman was a dermatologist and I was a cardiothoracic surgeon. No two medical specialities could be more different. We never met professionally. We worked at different hospitals. And yet we were good friends.

We met socially.

Kalman and I had a lot in common. The culture we'd been raised in was European (neither of us went to school in Britain) and, like me, Kalman loved medical science. This, for a dermatologist, was unusual. In the 1970's, most dermatologists had no interest in research – and many still don't!

Above all, we were both passionate about classical music. I'd studied at the conservatoire, and played violin; Kalman didn't play an instrument, but he could instantly name both the key and opus number of any Beethoven trio or quartet, and *never got it wrong.*

He spent much time and effort inveigling the local doctors to come to his musical evenings, but it was no good. They weren't interested and, after two years, he threw in the towel.

I don't know much about his background except that, after the Nazi occupation, he escaped from Hungary and, after many struggles, got himself and his wife into Britain.

He studied medicine in Glasgow, and worked in various posts, before becoming a consultant dermatologist in Hull in the late 1960s

Like me, Kalman was very happy in Britain, even though many of his medical colleagues didn't have a welcoming attitude. They were not xenophobic (at least, not openly), but they thought their overseas colleagues were more popular than they were, and they didn't like that.

I don't think we were really more popular. It just appeared that way because, being foreign, Kalman and I were more exotic – so we attracted more attention.

Kalman was also resented, by some, because not only was he good at his work, but he was also charismatic. He had an impeccable bedside manner, a charming accent, and a sexy huskiness in his voice that cast a spell – especially on the ladies.

Kalman did so well that he annoyed even the most prosperous of physicians – many of whom spent too much time looking over the fence to see who had the most successful private practice.

This story is about an incident that happened circa 1980.

At that time, consultant surgeons were provided with theatre gear – white shirts, white trousers, and surgical caps. When I first arrived at Castle Hill Hospital, I was measured by a tailor, which was followed by my being presented with a stack of short-sleeved monogrammed shirts, and well-fitting trousers.

Over the years, these trousers grew tighter, affecting my groin. By the end of a long day (which could last until 10 pm), I'd usually sweated quite a bit, which produced, over time, an itchy skin lesion at the top of my thigh and perineum.[16]

To begin with, I treated it myself but, after a week or so, it became so irksome that I telephoned Kalman at Hull Royal Infirmary.

"Look, why don't you come in and see me tomorrow?" he said.

"I can't. I'm operating, and can't leave Castle Hill until very late."

In the end, we worked out a time for him to see me.

When I arrived at the hospital, he was finishing his ward rounds. He was at the last patient's bed, surrounded by his junior staff, and two nurses.

[16] The space between the anus and scrotum.

He saw me and asked one of the nurses to take me to his office to wait.

After a short time, he arrived, relaying instructions to his registrar, who was scurrying behind him, and accompanied by a senior nurse, in a well-starched apron with a shiny silver belt buckle, who oozed authority and a mature sexuality.

I stood up to greet him with a 'continental hug' – which was our custom.

Kalman then asked the sister if we could please have a pot of tea and some biscuits. In those days, many consultants had a tray of tea after their ward rounds.

While the sister was out, Kalman asked me to show him the area of concern. I stood up and dropped my trousers. I should add here that, during the autumn and winter, I wore a three-piece suit, with a pocket watch and chain, and a flower in my lapel.

Picture the scene: me standing in full 'consultant's regalia,' with my trousers round my ankles and Kalman kneeling in front of me, with a torch in one hand, holding my testicles away from my thigh, and peering intently at my perineum.

The office door opened and the sister walked in with a tray of tea. The poor woman – totally embarrassed – swiftly left the room. There was a crash as the tray hit the floor. In her haste, she'd put the tray, unsafely, on a trolley of case records.

Kalman and I were briefly distracted, but not really disturbed. Afterwards, we found it hilarious.

I hadn't recalled this incident until recently, when I went to Kalman's funeral service. I was deeply upset at losing my dear friend, and the service was very solemn.

Then, out of nowhere, the memory of this incident popped into my head and it made me smile. I looked up, almost expecting to see Kalman grinning down at me from Heaven.

It was just like Kalman to cheer me up like that.

9

PIGEON-CHESTED IN GRIMSBY

Stanley was a fit, muscular man from Grimsby with a *pectus carinatum* (pigeon chest.)

He lived with his girlfriend and their young daughter in a council flat in Grimsby, and made his living on the docks, and on building sites.

I first met him on one of my fortnightly visits to Grimsby, where I ran a clinic at an old sanatorium called the Spring Field Clinic.

As a 25-year-old male with a chest deformity, Stanley was not on the top of my list for treatment. My policy was to give priority to children and young women. So, when I saw Stanley's name, I asked the Sister: "Who had the brilliant idea of putting him on my outpatients' list?"

But my attitude changed when I read his GP's notes. Because of his chest, Stanley had been bullied at school, and called 'Pigeon Chest Stan.' As a result, he'd taken up body-building to defend himself.

Even now, as an adult, he was still the target of verbal abuse because of his deformity.

'As a child, he was beaten up by the bigger boys,' wrote the GP. 'Now, he beats up anyone who teases him about his chest.'

Stanley had been up before the Magistrate several times on charges of assault. His last arrest had been for breaking the nose a man who'd called him a "pigeon-chested ape."

For this, he'd been given a suspended sentence. The Magistrate warned him that the next time he was in court, he would go to jail.

The last paragraph of the GP's letter said: 'I have known Stan since his childhood and am sure that by repairing his misshapen chest we can prevent his being locked up. I honestly believe the only way to keep this man out of prison, and save his family, is reconstructive surgery.'

The police reports (forwarded by his GP) described Stanley as a 'violent thug with a short fuse.' Nonetheless, I decided to see him.

At the interview, I was surprised to find him both articulate and mild-mannered. He didn't fit the picture in the police reports at all.

I examined him.

He had a severe chest deformity of long standing, which had affected his spine, making him slightly hunch-backed.

I placed his name on my urgent waiting list and, thanks to

a cancellation, was able to admit him quite quickly.

Correcting his chest was no easy task, and I wasn't entirely satisfied with my work. However, Stanley – who proved to be the perfect patient – was very pleased with the results.

Later, a colleague told me she'd seen Stanley showing off his chest at the local swimming pool.

For the next six years, I saw Stanley for check-ups. And, during all that time, he didn't get into a single fight, and wasn't seen in the Magistrate's Court.

What's more, he got married to his girlfriend, and they had a second child.

10

THE LOCUM

In October 1989, a registrar at my cardiothoracic centre, took a leave of absence to attend his father's funeral, and deal with family business.

We needed someone to fill in for him.

We needed a locum.

After looking at several candidates, we engaged a young African doctor, named Mr. Bagayogo.

Mr. Bagayogo was highly recommended. He'd completed his training in general surgery, and passed the Royal College of Surgeons examination, which made him an FRCS – a Fellow of the Royal College of Surgeons.

Furthermore, during his training, he'd worked for 6 months at a high-profile thoracic surgery unit in Scotland.

At the interview, Mr. Bagayogo told us he was returning to his own country in six weeks' time. For him, this was good timing. He could fill in for us prior to his departure.

We all heaved a huge sigh of relief. We were very fortunate to have filled the vacancy so quickly with such a good candidate.

In the days that followed, the whole team was impressed by Mr. Bagayogo's technical ability, and by how well he clicked with the other members of staff.

One weekend, an elderly patient named Mr. Harding was being visited by his wife and family. Mr. Harding had lung cancer, and I'd warned the family of its likely fatal outcome.

When they saw him, they became alarmed. Despite being on oxygen, his breathing was extremely laboured, and he was barely conscious. He appeared to be dying.

They urgently wanted to see a doctor.

Mr. Bagayogo, who was on duty that evening, came to answer their questions. He told them not to worry.

"He's all right," he said. "There's really no need to stay at the hospital. Go home and get some rest."

So, the family went home.

The next morning, Mrs. Harding got a call from the hospital. Her husband had passed away in the night.

She was devastated.

She rushed to the hospital and demanded to see Bagayogo.

Later, I learned that Mr. and Mrs. Harding had rarely been apart. They'd been sweethearts since their teens and, in the seaside village where they lived, they were known for always walking hand-in-hand. I could well imagine how terrible she must have felt, not being there at her husband's death-bed.

Our locum registrar had been up late the previous night, dealing with an emergency admission. Starved of sleep, he was reluctant to get out of bed for the family of a dead patient, so he asked the night sister if she could handle the situation.

But Mrs. Harding wouldn't accept this. And neither would her children, who had joined her at the hospital. They insisted on seeing Mr. Bagayogo.

So, he rose from his bed, got dressed, and made his way to the ward.

Although not happy to be there, he kept his composure, and listened, good-naturedly, to the accusations and complaints of Mrs. Harding and her family.

When they were finished, he said: "Well, I'm awfully sorry to tell you but, with the best will in the world, people do sometimes bump off, you know."

At this, the family exploded, and only the intervention of a nurse stopped Mr. Bagayogo from being physically assaulted.

By early afternoon, I had a four-page letter from Mrs. Harding, and an official letter from the hospital administrator, asking me to intercede.

I began by speaking to Mr. Bagayogo.

I listened to his side of the story, and then advised him to write a letter.

In his letter, he apologised to the family, and his words included the following:

'I saw that Mrs. Harding was exhausted and that she wanted to go home and have a restful night.'

Next, I invited the family to my office. I told them I was very sorry for the distress they'd been caused by the doctor's error of judgement, but assured them that the doctor had not been negligent, or failing in his duty towards his patient. No doubt, he'd been unwise in advising the family to go home, but it was an honest mistake. He had no way of knowing Mr. Harding was going to pass away, and he was concerned about the family spending an uncomfortable night at the hospital.

But nothing I said could quell the family's outrage at his use of the term 'bump off.'

I agreed that his use of language was unwise, but asked them to forgive him because he'd been working late the night before, and his poor choice of words was due to fatigue.

Eventually, the family's fury subsided, and they accepted my apologies.

We all shook hands.

Before leaving our hospital, the young Mr. Bagayogo came to see me.

"Well sir," he said. "I'm off now, and I have come to thank you. Working here has been a bloody good experience. And

I have also learned a very important lesson here – something they did not teach me at the College of Surgeons."

"And what is that?" I asked him.

"How to manage the delicate sensitivities of the family of a patient who has bumped off."

11

DEATH AND THE MAIDEN

I first heard the string quartet, *Death and the Maiden,* by Franz Schubert, in 1947. But I don't think I truly understood it until 30 years later, through the death of a friend.

Not long after my arrival in Hull, a weekly, multi-disciplinary meeting was established to discuss patients who might need cardiac surgery. At one of these meetings, we discussed a female who'd been seen at Rheumatology because of pains in the joints of her hands.

There were chest X-rays, taken when she was 14, showing a growth between the lungs.[17] This had been diagnosed as a benign cyst. The cardiologists and radiologists felt that, as the cyst had been there for 10 years without change, there was no need for an investigation. I disagreed. I knew that cysts of the mediastinum could exist for many years before changing into malignant tumours.

I believe my colleagues thought I had 'happy knife syndrome' (a dig aimed at over-enthusiastic surgeons), and

[17] An area known as the mediastinum.

no-one backed my opinion.

Two years later, I had an emergency referral. A woman with arthritis in her hands, who was coughing up blood.

After reading her notes, I asked to see her X-rays. Studying them on the viewing box, they looked familiar. They were the same ones I'd seen at the team meeting, two years before.

The patient's name was Jennifer Jones. She was 25 years old, born in Aberystwyth, Wales, had a degree in Zoology, and was married to a man named Paul. She had three young children – two boys and a girl.

When she entered my consulting room, what I saw was a skinny young woman, with dark hair, lustrous eyes, and the limp body-language of the defeated.

"Are you Mrs Jennifer Jones?"

She spoke so softly, I couldn't hear her reply.

"Excuse me?"

"Yes, I am," she said.

She was barely audible.

I asked her about her medical history, leaning forward so I could hear her.

"For the past 14 months," she said slowly, her eyes welling with tears, "I've been seen by lots of doctors...and no-one's told me what's wrong with me." The tears ran quietly down her cheeks. "All they do is keep changing my medication."

I was furious. I knew there was a chance she had a tumour, which could well be malignant. I couldn't tell her this, though, which made it all the more frustrating.

Then I examined her.

Her fingers had a 'drumstick' shape, and her fingernails had a deformity known as 'clubbing.'

I'd first learned about this in Geneva, during the last year of my medical studies. One afternoon, the celebrated pathologist, Professor Erwin Rutishauser, was inspecting a post-mortem I'd done. He asked for my findings, and the cause of death.

This was a case of lung cancer, which I'd gone to great lengths to research.

The professor asked if I'd looked at the cadaver's hands.

"I am sorry, Monsieur, I did not."

I'd been so engrossed in the lung cancer, that I hadn't noticed changes in the fingers and fingernails.

"Well, look at them now, and tell me what you see."

"They are deformed. Did the deceased have arthritis?"

"Not necessarily," replied Rutis (his students called him Rutis) "We call this *Doigts en baton de tombour.*" [18]

When I examined Jenny's hands, Rutis's voice sprang into

[18] Drumstick fingers.

my head. "Regardez Monsieur, qu'est ce que vous voyez?"

My God. She had *doigts en baton de tombour!*

"Are you all right, sir?" asked my assistant.

"I'm fine. Look at Mrs. Jones's fingers. Do you see anything special about them?"

"Yes, sir. Characteristics of osteoarthritis."

"Not necessarily. We call this 'drumstick fingers' – and the curved nails are known as 'clubbing of the fingernails.'"

Jenny perked up. "It started about two years ago," she said. "I saw my doctor, and a specialist, and they both said it was arthritis."

This was a misdiagnosis. But, to make sure, I needed to do a bronchoscopy. [19]

I carried this out, and found compression from outside the bronchial tube, reducing the calibre of one of the major branches of the bronchi by 50%.

There had to be a large tumour narrowing the lumen.

I sent Jenny to Radiology for a new set of X-rays. The X-rays confirmed a mediastinal tumour. She was admitted to my ward and prepared for surgery.

This was a major – and complex – operation. I had to

[19] A bronchoscope is inserted, usually through the nose or mouth, which allows the doctor to examine the patient's airways for abnormalities such as foreign bodies, bleeding, tumours, or inflammation.

open the chest from the front, and from the side, and divide the breastbone from top to bottom.

But everything went well. I found the tumour (which had entered the left lung) and, to remove it, I excised a portion of the upper part of the lung, and part of the pericardium.[20]

The tumour went to be analysed and, as I'd feared, it was malignant. The question now was: had cancer cells spread to other parts of the body?

I looked into the possibility of chemotherapy and radiation, but was advised to 'hold tight.' My complete removal of the tumour may have done the trick.

A follow-up was scheduled and, a month later, I saw Jenny at my outpatients' clinic.

She came in looking the very picture of health. I examined her and, pleased with her progress, arranged to see her 3 months later.

Before leaving my office, she stopped and said: "Can I ask your advice on something?"

"Of course."

"It's rather awkward. I'm not sure where to start."

"The beginning's usually a good place."

"Okay. Some time back, after the birth of my third child,

[20] The sac membrane enclosing the heart.

Paul and I decided not to have any more children."

She glanced at me, to see if I disapproved.

I nodded for her to continue.

"After a lot of talking about it – about all the different types of contraceptives – Paul decided to have a vasectomy."

Again, she paused to get my reaction.

"Go on," I said.

"Then I got ill. And now he's changed his mind." She began to pace back and forth. "The funny thing is he won't say why. I keep asking him, but he doesn't want to talk about it. So, I feel it's down to me. I have to do something. I don't want to get pregnant again."

She stopped pacing, and took a deep breath. "What do you think about sterilisation?"

"Sterilisation? Well, you're fit enough."

She smiled with relief.

"Is that what you wanted to know?"

"Yes, thank you. My GP wasn't sure about it." She paused. "He also told me there's a long waiting list for the operation."

"What does your husband think about it?"

"Oh, he's fine with it." She looked at me with her large soulful eyes. "I was wondering if you knew anyone who might be able to do it?"

Actually, I *did* know someone – a consultant gynaecologist

who owed me a favour.

"Possibly. But I'm not making any promises. I'll see what I can do."

A year before, I'd been called, in a panic, to the Maternity Wing of a hospital on the outskirts of the city. One of their patients was having a difficult labour, and was showing signs of hypoxia.[21]

The consultant gynaecologist believed there was a danger of pulmonary embolus – where a blood clot is dislodged and moves into the lung. This can be life-threatening.

The gynaecologist had heard there was a new chest surgeon in the area, found my number, and called me.

I drove as fast as I could to the hospital and, when I arrived, I saw the patient lying in an eccentric position on the bed, starting to turn blue.

I looked at the chest X-ray. It appeared normal, but had been taken using a portable machine, which has low resolution.

I asked the sister to fetch the biggest syringe they had, as quickly as possible. The patient was in great distress, and I was worried about the effects of oxygen deficiency on her unborn child.

[21] Insufficiency of oxygen.

I inserted the needle into the patient's chest.

As soon as the needle went in, the plunger almost blew out of the syringe. The air was under enormous pressure inside the chest. I removed the plunger, let the air escape, and asked for two sterile tubes (urinary catheters), a bowl of water, and a surgical scalpel.

When these were produced, I inserted one of the tubes into the patient's chest, connected it to the second tube, and put the end of the second tube under the water in the bowl, which I placed below the level of the patient's chest.

Bubbles of air churned in the water.

The patient's colour improved, her breathing normalised, and she was encouraged to push.

Ten minutes later, the baby was born – a little baby girl who was blue and not breathing. The midwife gave her a smack on her bottom. This was followed by a cry – the baby took a breath – and her skin turned from blue to pink.

I rang my own hospital and, after less than an hour, my assistant brought me the equipment I needed to thoroughly drain the mother's chest.

What had happened was the strain of pushing, during delivery, had burst a small part of the patient's lung, causing air to escape into the chest cavity, which had made the lung collapse. When this happened, the mother and her unborn baby were deprived of oxygen.

A few days later, I carried out an operation to seal the air leak, and everything was fine. The gynaecologist declared my actions 'heroic', sent me a bottle of wine, and told me he owed me a favour.

To get back to Jenny, I decided to call in the favour.

My gynaecologist colleague was sympathetic, and Jenny didn't wait long for her operation.

Three months went by, and I received a letter from her. In it, she said her children had started school, and she needed to do something with her brain. Could she volunteer to help me in my research work?

Naturally, I was dubious, but she was so persuasive that I let her join my research team for a few hours, twice a week, to see how she'd handle it.

She took to it like a duck to water. She had the critical thinking skills necessary for scientific work, and revelled in the atmosphere of clinical research.

In fact, as time went on, I began to depend on her.

Over the following six months, we almost doubled our research output, our journal publications, and our scientific and clinical presentations.

In 1975, I became interested in the teaching of nurses, and wrote articles for the nursing magazines. I did this because, at that time, the training of nurses in thoracic surgery was barely adequate.

Jenny was very encouraging, and helpful, in this effort.

Another one of our projects involved nutrition. In the 1970's and early '80s, there was great interest in finding ways to deliver complete parenteral nutrition[22] to patients who couldn't take food by mouth.

Academic surgery units – notably Newcastle and Sheffield University Hospitals – had vastly superior laboratories and research personnel to mine, but they didn't have access to as many patients with swallowing issues as I did.

In 1976, I planned a nursing book, and also a European Club for thoracic surgery. Jenny, despite her young age, was an excellent, and enthusiastic, sounding board.

In January 1977, as part of her 4-monthly check-up, I sent her to have an X-ray and, as was routine at the time, to bring the film back for me to review.

Unexpectedly, when I looked at the X-ray, I saw a small tumour in the right lung.

My expression must have given me away.

"It's back, isn't it?" said Jenny.

"I am afraid it looks that way, yes."

[22] Intravenous feeding.

"Can I sit down?"

"Yes, of course."

"Have you any brandy or whisky?"

I produced a bottle, and she had a stiff drink. There followed a long silence.

I sat down beside her and took her hand. "What about Paul, would you like me to talk to him?"

"No thank you. I'll tell him."

That night I hardly slept.

The next morning, I met with the pathologist who'd reported on the excised tumour, the radiotherapist, my anaesthetist, and a physician friend, to form a multidisciplinary team to tackle Jenny's condition.

The prevailing opinion was a short course of radiotherapy, followed by surgical excision of the tumour.

The radiotherapy took place towards the end of January 1977.

In mid-February, I carried out the operation. I removed the tumour, but found multiple small tumours in the chest wall, lung, pleura, and wall of the heart.

Now, we were truly cornered. Nevertheless, I was determined to reduce, or stop, the spread of the cancer.

I was advised to start her on a long course of chemotherapy – even though there were no specific drugs for the type of cancer she had. Also, Jenny was against toxic drugs, with nasty side effects, whose results were uncertain.

I was desperately worried, so I consulted a friend of mine in Leeds – one of the top chemo-radiotherapists in the country.

After a quick call, he asked me to come and see him, and bring Jenny, and all the relevant information.

At the end of our visit, after careful consideration, our joint decision was to keep going, for as long as possible, without treatment.

Driving back towards Hull, Jenny and I took a country road and, when we were about 10 miles out from Leeds, we entered a patch of woodland. She asked me to stop the car.

She got out, and wandered into the woods. Then she turned and beckoned me to follow. So, I did.

After a short walk, she bent down, picked up a beetle, and placed it in the palm of her hand.

"This is a male stag beetle," she said. "It lives underground until this time of year, when it comes to the surface to mate."

I knew nothing about the life cycle of the stag beetle – or any other beetle – but Jenny, the zoologist, was in her element.

"A few weeks after mating, it dies," she said.

Towards mid-June, she developed more secondary

tumours. We had to take action. The cancer was spreading. The consensus was chemotherapy – what I call 'the atomic bomb of cancer-therapy.' In those days, chemotherapy didn't distinguish between friend or foe. It destroyed good cells as well as bad.

Jenny became debilitated, and lost her appetite, and her hair. But she didn't want to stop working. We arranged it so she could work at home. The only times she came to the hospital were for intravenous nutrition.

Our research on artificial nutrition progressed and – inspired by Jenny – I designed an intravenous device to allow patients to receive nutrients at home, even when they were moving about. Also, the feeding device could be stopped, plugged off, and restarted whenever convenient.

Thanks to Jenny's need for this device – and her unflagging willingness to test it – we ironed out all the kinks, and gained optimum function.

I later published the invention, and its methodology, in the journal of the Royal College of Surgeons of Edinburgh.[23] I should have patented it, but never did. Others – mostly Americans – commercialised it, and it's now used throughout the world.

[23] A Technique of Superior Vena Caval Catheterisation for Prolonged Intravenous Feeding. **Moghissi** K. J R CollSurgEdinb. **1979** May 24(3): 178-9.)

Despite her anaemia, frequent blood transfusions, and hair loss, Jenny amazed me by how good she looked. She was as skilled with wigs, and make-up, as she was in her research work.

By the end of July, chemotherapy became ineffective, her analgesics [24] had to be changed frequently, and Jenny's GP was having trouble dealing with her suffering.

I received a letter asking me to visit her.

As I entered her room, on the first floor of her house, she sat up in bed, looking luminous, and said: "Why don't you send me any more work?"

I started to tell her I was respecting her privacy – but she stopped me.

"There's nothing wrong with my brain!"

"All right, all right," I said. "You're on. Would you like me to come and see you three times a week, for a couple of hours in the evening, to work on the book?"

One of the projects I'd put on hold, due to lack of time, was the book on thoracic surgical nursing, which Jenny had been helping with. She'd been doing the anatomical drawings, but had to stop when she fell ill.

"That would be the best medication I could ever have!"

[24] Painkillers.

The next day, on her instructions, I bought special paper, Indian ink, a divider, and two drawing pens.

When I delivered them, she handed me a letter from her GP.

"Dear Mr Moghissi,

I am most grateful to you for giving my patient, Jenny, a new lease of life... I have left some empty prescription forms that I've signed. Please write any drug you feel appropriate for her needs. I will continue to see her weekly.

Yours..."

'What a good doctor!' I thought.

In the event, with no more chemo, Jenny's appetite came back, and she needed less painkillers to help her sleep.

We made progress with the book, and I found a publisher.

One day in her room, watching her as she dozed off, I decided to sit quietly and write on the subject of caring for patients with disseminated thoracic neoplasia.[25]

Here's an extract:

"The inevitability of death in patients with carcinomatosis, should not detract the medical and nursing staff's attention from the care they require. The fact that these patients are in hospital, or in an acute medical or surgical ward, should not let the routine

[25] Cancer.

of life-saving machinery override their right to die peacefully. Patients with disseminated growth should be helped mentally and physically to an acceptable death, free from pain, fear and suffering.

The philosophy and attitude that "nothing can be done for these patients" should be condemned. The aim of the treatment is obviously not to cure but to reduce suffering, and to offer the patient a better quality of life.

With this in mind, a lot can be done for them.

Active resuscitative measures in a terminal cancer case should not be pursued, as there is no more horrifying spectacle than that of an eager nursing and medical team jumping on the chest of such patients for the purpose of cardiac massage – nor is artificial ventilation justifiable when their respiration is failing.

It is clear, therefore, that there must be a balance between treatment to relieve pain, on the one hand, and exhaustive invasive examinations which can induce unnecessary suffering, on the other..."[26]

While I was writing, Jenny woke up, and asked what I was doing. I said I was getting on with the book for nurses.

"You *must* finish it!" she rasped, her eyes wide.

I promised I would.

[26] K. Moghissi. Chapter 30: Care of Patients with Disseminated Thoracic Neoplasia; in Thoracic Surgery For Nurses. K.Moghissi, Kimpton Medical London 1982: pp 291-95.

Jenny was now living one day at a time – not knowing if she'd be alive the next day.

But she made it to her birthday.

How do you say 'Happy Birthday' to an intelligent young woman who's terminally ill with cancer? And what would be a suitable present for such a young lady? A few more pain killers? Flowers that could be later used at her funeral?

As I drove through the twisting country roads, back from my clinic at Scarborough, I was tortured with sadness and anger.

I took a number of detours to make the journey last longer and, at one point, noticed a profusion of wildflowers at the side of the road. I pulled in, parked the car, got out, and started picking.

I didn't know the names of the flowers. The red ones looked like rosebay, the yellow ones, buttercups or celandines. Some of the foliage may have been wild lavender. There were daisies, poppies, and some small flowers that looked like raindrops, which may have been wild orchids.

Each time I cut a stem, a little fluid trickled out. This made me feel culpable. But I felt sure the flowers wouldn't mind being sacrificed to bring a moment of happiness to a wonderful young woman who was dying.

I put the flowers together in a bundle, fastened them with straw, and drove to Jenny's house.

The children were in the sitting room, preparing a small birthday party for their mother. Paul, her husband, was still at work.

My arrival in her room, with the wildflowers, made her smile.

"Thank you," she said, with difficulty – she was very short of breath. "This is the best present I could have for my last birthday. I wish I had something to give you."

Then she said: "Did you do anything to my heart when you were operating and manipulating things in my chest?"

"No, there was nothing wrong with your heart."

"You must have touched it during the operation."

"Of course I did."

"That must have been when I gave it to you."

Trying not to break down, I sat on her bed, and gently held her hand. She closed her eyes, visibly exhausted.

After a few moments, she whispered something that sounded like 'good night.'

I waited for a while and then, when I was sure she was asleep, I quietly left the room.

She died two days later.

12

WHITEHALL

Surgical Staplers can be used instead of sutures (stitches) to connect parts of the bowel, staple lung tissue together, and close skin wounds and surgical incisions.

Initially, these staplers were very cumbersome and only used in gastric surgery to place two rows of sutures, which allowed the surgeon to cut in-between them without the contents of the stomach leaking out.

Modern staplers first appeared in the 1970's and, by the late 1980's, medical device companies were producing dozens of new ones for every purpose imaginable.

I was one of the first to remove a pulmonary nodular lesion[27] with the help of a stapler, which I did in order to evaluate the stapler's efficiency and cost effectiveness.

In 1990, I requested a new type of stapler that came with reloadable cartridges.

At the time, political change was in the air (again), just as we were at the tail-end of an earlier major reorganisation.

[27] A small, diseased round or oval-shaped growth in the lung.

Since the mid-80's, governments have persistently tried to interfere with the National Health Service – and have often succeeded!

Two months had passed since my request for the stapler, and I was getting impatient.

One morning, I'd had enough.

I asked my registrar to close the patient's chest, left the operating theatre, took off my clogs, put on outside shoes and a white coat, and marched to the Manager's office.

We had a name for our hospital's administration department. We called it 'Whitehall.'

The hospital manager was a nice enough chap, always striving to adjust to the changing winds that blew from the Department of Health. The gyrations he performed in order to please his masters often made life hard for the doctors, nurses and patients, yet he was approachable, and not the type of boffin you needed to make an appointment to see.

But, on that day, he wasn't in his office.

His secretary said: "Is there anything I can help you with?"

"Can you remind your boss to call me, please? It's two months since I requested a stapler, and I've heard nothing."

"Your requisition is still in his tray," she said. "He's thinking about it."

"Thinking about it? What's to think about?"

"Well, he thought the stapler you asked for was too expensive. What's wrong with having a stapler like the one we have here?"

I couldn't believe what I was hearing.

So, I spent the next five minutes explaining the difference between an office stapler and a surgical stapler.

Unlike many stories involving hospital management, this one has a happy ending.

Two weeks after I visited 'Whitehall,' I received my stapler – and it wasn't from Ryman's!

13

FARMER'S LUNG

In 1956, I became a Registrar in Thoracic Surgery at the Victoria Hospital in Blackpool.

This elevation had happened quickly. I'd only been a house surgeon at Nottingham University Hospital for ten months, and it was just two years since my first job, as a junior house surgeon, at Edgware Hospital, in London.

I was scheduled to start work at the start of September, but this coincided with the birth of my son.

So, I asked my bosses in Blackpool if I could delay it until October.

This was agreed and thus, a week before the beginning of October, my wife, myself, our 3-week-old son, and all our belongings, were crammed into my small Ford Prefect car.

What didn't help matters was I had a fever, caused by an angry boil on the back of my neck.

We had planned to stay at the hospital, but this turned out to be impossible because of the cries of our new-born baby. However, to our great good fortune, my wife, Alex, had an aunt who lived in Blackpool – a wonderful woman –

who let us camp at her house.

Aunty Madge was an attractive 60-year-old, with a peachy complexion and a tremendous pair of legs – which she wasn't shy about showing off. During WWII, she'd worked at an American army base in the south of England, and had many fond memories!

Madge was very kind-hearted and had a terrific sense of humour – just the type of person you need when you're under stress. She settled us into her spare room and, in less than a week, I was recovered, and ready to start work.

My year at the Victoria Hospital was invaluable. It was here that I learned to do most of the standard chest operations.

My senior consultant was a tall, handsome, Aberdonian Scot, in his late forties, named John Stuart Glennie. He had a pleasing accent, and a charming manner, and was popularly known as 'J.S.'

One of the many things J.S. trained me in was the surgery of pulmonary tuberculosis.

I'd always been keen on tuberculosis. My first exposure to it had been as a student, when I'd visited the TB sanatoria in Leysin and Montana in Switzerland.

Later, at Nottingham University Hospital, I was introduced to the surgical aspects of tuberculosis – although this happened more by accident than design.

The accident was that one of my chiefs in Nottingham had a non-fatal heart attack.

Before his coronary, he used to drive to a sanatorium in Grantham to hold an outpatients' clinic, and do operations. After the heart attack, he continued with this work, but adopted two strategies to minimise his workload. First, he limited his repertoire of tuberculosis treatments to one – *thoracoplasty*.

(Thoracoplasty is the excision of ribs on the side where the lung is damaged by tuberculosis. After the ribs are removed, the lung collapses, which helps it to heal.)

His second strategy was to take me with him.

At first, I thought he wanted me to be his assistant. But that wasn't quite what he had in mind. Thoracoplasty can be a very physically exhausting procedure. He wanted me to do the operations.

He would change into his theatre gear, scrub up, and sit on the surgeon's stool, while I did the work under his watchful eye. All he did was put his hand in the wound at the beginning, and at the end, of the procedure, to record that he'd 'done the operation.'

I didn't mind this, because I gained a lot of experience.

Being interested in tuberculosis, and knowing that J.S. went each Monday to a sanatorium to operate on patients with TB, I made him a proposition. If I did all my Monday ward work on Sunday, would he let me accompany him to the sanatorium on Monday?

He agreed.

So, that's how I began going, with my much-admired chief, to High Carley Sanatorium in Ulverston.

To get there, we started at 7 a.m., travelling in J.S.'s red Jaguar, with the consultant anaesthetist sitting beside him in the front.

I was jammed in the back, with a mass of case records, which I'd spent the previous night reading.

I'd make a résumé of these records, so I could recite the details when we saw the patients before the operation. I wanted to impress – and I think it worked!

During the journey, the back seat of the 1956 Jag would rock from side to side when the car rounded a corner. I'll never forget the winding avenues, and spectacular scenery, as we roared over carpets of fallen leaves, making them dance and shimmer in the exhaust of the car.

Once a month, after finishing work at High Carley, J.S. drove to Grange-over-Sand, on Morecombe Bay, to one of the UK's first-ever sanatoria.

It was here that J.S. conducted a short outpatients' clinic.

The first time I went there, he asked me, as we entered

the sanatorium grounds, if I knew of a condition called 'Farmer's Lung.'

"I've heard of it," I said. "It's caused by a fungal infection, isn't it?"

He said that was about right, and asked if I knew who'd discovered it.

"I think it was Löffler. Wilhelm Löffler, the Swiss physician who described 'Löffler's Syndrome.'"[28]

He smiled, said nothing, but there was a twinkle in his eye.

We got out of the car, crunched up the gravel drive, climbed a few marble steps, and entered the grand foyer of the Victorian sanatorium. Here, we were met by an elderly, white-haired doctor, in a white coat.

J.S. introduced him as Dr. Campbell, and told him I was his new registrar, "whose knowledge is much above those I've had before. He even knows about Farmer's Lung!"

He then turned to me and said: "This is Dr Campbell who first described Farmer's Lung in 1932."

Now I understood the twinkle.

Dr. Campbell asked if I'd like to see the original X-rays of Farmer's Lung, and hear about the history and presentation of the first patient.

[28] Pneumonia caused by a parasitic infection.

Naturally, I said 'yes.'

We went down a flight of dark stairs to a cold, underground room, where hundreds of packs of X-rays were arranged, and catalogued, on shelves.

Dr. Campbell moved about the shelves picking up one envelope after another and muttering to himself: "No, not this one. Not this one..."

Then his face lit up. "Here it is!"

He fished out a voluminous pack of X-rays and put two of them on the viewing box. Full of enthusiasm, he looked years younger than he had a few minutes before, up on the ground floor.

He then related, in detail, how he'd detected what became known as Farmer's Lung. I've never forgotten the experience, and I can still see, in my mind's eye, those first, historical X-ray images.

Back in the 1950's, we didn't have computers. If we wanted information, we had to go to the library. So, it took me a few months before I found Dr. Campbell's original publication, and learned more about Farmer's Lung.

Interestingly, Dr. Campbell and Wilhelm Löffler (who I'd thought had first described the condition) both made their important discoveries in the same year – 1932.

A note on Pulmonary Tuberculosis and Sanatoria: Until the mid 20th century, Pulmonary Tuberculosis (TB) was one of the worst killers of humanity. Before the discovery of antibiotics, treatments for TB included the inhaling of smouldering cow dung, and 'Regal Touching.'[29] In other words, hopeless.

In 1854, Hermann Brehmer, a German doctor with TB, was advised by his professor to find a healthier climate. He went to the Himalayas and – amazingly – returned home cured.

This showed that tuberculosis was curable. And, it also inspired Dr Brehmer to invent the world's first sanatorium – a re-creation of his Himalayan retreat – where patients could enjoy fresh air, exercise, and nutritious food.

The results achieved by his sanatorium far surpassed all previous attempts to treat the disease, and it wasn't long before others followed his example, and sanatoria began appearing all over Europe and America.

These sanatoria provided a dual function: 1) they protected the general population by isolating the infected, and 2) they gave patients a healthy lifestyle, which boosted their immune systems, and assisted their recovery.

And it was in these sanatoria that the first surgical treatments of pulmonary tuberculosis were developed.

[29] People believed they could be cured of TB if they were touched by a king.

14

WINNIE

Winnie was a glamorous, 77-year-old ex-cabaret artiste, who lived in a bungalow in a small village near Hull.

"Do you know why they call it a bungalow?" she asked me, one day.

"No, I don't."

"It's because, Kevin, (she always called me Kevin[30]) a man was once building a house and he got tired. So, he said to his mates: 'Let's not bother with a second storey. Let's *bung a low* roof on it."

She liked to tell jokes. When I once asked her about her diet, she replied: "Seafood. I see food and I eat it."

Winnie had a nice, old-fashioned GP whose medical approach to the elderly was to treat their aches and pains with a plethora of pills and potions.

We got along well – the GP and I – but he didn't think much of surgeons. He often said: "The problem with surgeons is their answer to everything is to *cut it out.*"

[30] My first name is Keyvan.

One morning, Winnie coughed up a large amount of blood. Her GP called to ask my opinion.

"You don't need my opinion, doctor," I said. "You need to call a bloody ambulance!"

When she arrived at the hospital, it was about 10.30 a.m., and I'd just finished my first operation of the day.

I sent Winnie to Radiology.

Her X-ray revealed a large hiatal hernia. Most of her stomach was in her chest cavity.

I carried out a gastroscopy[31] and found a bleeding ulcer, which I quickly cauterised. Then I opened the left chest and pushed her stomach back into its correct place in the abdomen.

Next, I repaired the hole through which the stomach had escaped into the chest, and completed the operation by stitching up the incision.

Winnie had a strong diaphragm and good muscle-tone – no doubt the result of a lifetime of singing and dancing. Her recovery was swift.

And, a week later, she was on her way home.

Over the next four years, Winnie visited my outpatients' clinic for quarterly check-ups. I always enjoyed seeing her.

[31] Looking into the interior of the stomach with an endoscope.

She would enter like an East Yorkshire version of Joan Collins or Tallulah Bankhead – an elderly star, radiating fun, glamour and glitz.

Three years after her operation, she sent me a photo taken at her 80th birthday party. On the back, she'd written:

The Five Men in My Life.
Patrick – my bank manager (retired): does gardening as hobby, brings me plants.
David – my agent at Thomas Cook & Co: looks after my holidays.
John – my interior decorator: does my decorating.
Carl – my toy-boy and bridge partner. I am proud he is only in his thirties.
Kevin – the only man I take my clothes off for.

15

NELSON MANDELA

It was the 5th of December, 2013, and I was on my way to Geneva.

I'd woken extra-early, at 5 a.m. My precious wife, Alex (who can never be out-done), was already up, preparing breakfast. According to Alex, no man can face the rigours of the day without first having a full English breakfast.

The radio was on in the kitchen, and a presenter was gabbling dire warnings of storms and chaos on the roads, so, when breakfast was over, I hopped on the Internet to see if the trains were still running.

Apparently, they were.

I drove to the station, left the car in the long-stay car park, and walked into the station concourse. It was unusually crowded.

It turned out the 7 a.m. train to London had been cancelled.

Then, *all* the trains to London were cancelled!

There was nothing I could do, so I got back in the car and drove home to reschedule my appointments, and make lots of apologetic phone calls.

Once this was done, I turned on the desktop computer, and checked the news.

Nelson Mandela had died.

Finding myself unpredictably at leisure, I put on one of my favourite pieces of music: Beethoven's Triple Concerto in C Major, for Violin, Cello and Piano.

I'd first heard this when I was a student, but hadn't owned a copy until the spring of 1972, when my friend Sharon gave me a cassette.

As I listened to the Trio, my mind sailed back to when I'd first met her. It was shortly after I'd started a research trial in intravenous feeding for patients with oesophageal cancer.

Sharon was then 30-years-old, attractive, well-educated, and newly-married. She worked as a rep for a French pharmaceutical company, and had come to my office to show me some drugs they were marketing.

In the course of our meeting, it emerged she was a pianist. I told her I played the violin. As she lived locally, we agreed to attempt a music session together. When we finally did this, it was fun. So, from time to time, we met to play music.

As time went on, it became obvious that Sharon had problems in her marriage. Although her husband, Rob, had graduated in mineralogy, and was admired for his achievements, he was very insecure. And he was frustrated at work.

This insecurity and frustration produced in him an unceasing fount of aggression. And he would release his aggression on Sharon.

Rob was a man who needed to dominate.

Early in 1976, Sharon asked if I knew anything about South Africa. She told me Rob was thinking of going to Johannesburg because there were more opportunities there for mineralogists.

Well, I didn't know much about South Africa, apart from the medical system as it related to cardiothoracic surgery. I knew about apartheid, of course. We all knew about that. And my feeling was she wouldn't like it there.

Sharon was a Hullion – born and bred in Hull – a free-thinking city whose Member of Parliament had once been William Wilberforce, the father of the anti-slavery movement.

Sharon agreed she'd most likely have some problems with apartheid, but was sure her husband wouldn't!

So, Sharon and Rob went to South Africa.

A few weeks after they left, I received a long letter recording everything that had happened since their arrival. She was already missing Hull and the UK.

Thereafter, she wrote to me every two or three weeks.

One of her letters described a road accident. A black

woman had been hurt crossing the road. Sharon gave her first-aid until the ambulance arrived. But the ambulance was for whites only and, when the driver saw the casualty was black, it sped off.

Sharon and the injured woman had to wait another half hour for the right ambulance (for blacks) to arrive.

All her letters expressed a desperation to leave South Africa, and come home. But she didn't do it.

Sometime later, she wrote saying she'd met an orthopaedic surgeon[32] who was an excellent pianist. This letter sounded more positive. I wondered if, at last, she was adjusting to being in South Africa.

It seemed she was, because her letters became shorter and less frequent.

Her next important letter announced she was pregnant by her husband.

Several months went by, and then, to my complete surprise, she showed up, unannounced, at my hospital – very pregnant, and radiant.

She couldn't stand South Africa any longer, she said, and she wasn't going to have her baby 'in that country.' She was back in England for good.

[32] Orthopedic surgeons treat conditions that affect the bones, joints, muscles, ligaments, tendons, and nerves.

Her husband was staying in Johannesburg, and she was going to divorce him.

Sharon found a nice flat in Hull, gave birth to a perfect baby girl, and the divorce went through.

As for Rob, he remained in South Africa, where he could be dominant because he was white. Did he stay after Nelson Mandela became President? I don't know. But I don't think he would have been too happy about that!

The third movement of the Concerto in C Major for Violin, Cello and Piano came to an end, and so did my trip down memory lane.

16

NO SAX HERE

Josh was smashed up in his car. As he was crossing a junction in his Fiat 500, he was hit by a big panel van, driven by a drunk driver.

He suffered head and chest injuries, and had multiple chest operations, and two emergency procedures to remove blood clots from inside his skull.

He also needed a tracheotomy so he could breathe.

A tracheotomy is the making of a small opening in the trachea (wind pipe) below the Adam's apple. A tube is placed in the upper airway and connected to the ventilator, providing the patient with artificial respiration.

Before the accident, Josh had been a cabinet-maker and an amateur saxophone player. At weekends, he played with his friends at parties and in local pubs.

But that all went south after the accident.

Here was a nice-looking, hard-working young man, with a rich social life, robbed of it all by a drunk driver. If only some of those who take the wheel after drinking could see the misery they cause!

Josh recovered, but it took some time, and he was left with brain-damage, and issues with his upper airway, which caused a cough so intense he spat blood.

Josh became my patient in the mid 1980's. By that time, I was experienced with lasers, and often used them to fix problems in the airway, and thereby avoid the need for major surgery.

I began Josh's treatment by using a laser to carefully dispose of the scar tissue that was causing an infected wound inside his trachea. After 4 treatments – each lasting about half an hour – the bleeding stopped. Now, he could breathe more easily. And cough much less.

To strengthen his trachea and lung function, I encouraged him to play the saxophone – which he did diligently – and, one year into his treatment, his breathing was 85% normal, and his cough had almost gone.

The only problem was that, when he played the sax, he played out of tune.

This is not unique. In the medical literature, you can find documented cases of string and woodwind players who, after a head injury, are unable to hear when they play wrong notes.

After about 18 months, Josh was in good physical shape but, because of his brain damage, he couldn't work as a cabinet maker.

But there was something he *could* do – busk.

When, during one of his treatment sessions, Josh told me he was busking, I was surprised because being a street performer demands courage, and his courage had been knocked sideways by the accident.

I asked if he was nervous playing in public.

"Nay," he said. "You gave me back me bottle."

"How's that?"

"It's me poster – what I put where I'm playin', see? Yer photo's on it. Gives me confidence, like."

I was mystified. What was he talking about?

I asked him where he was busking.

"Different places. Bradford, Bridlington, York – all over. Right now, I'm in Scarborough, outside Marks & Sparks."

The following Monday, after finishing my weekly clinic in Scarborough, I went to have a look at a men's outfitters, which I'd been told was good and reasonably priced.

After that, I drove towards the town centre, parked my car, and walked towards a restaurant run by an ex-patient of mine.

My plan was to have a quick lunch.

As I entered the main shopping centre, I heard an out-of-tune saxophone. I walked towards the sound, turned a corner and, for a moment, was dazzled by the sunlight. Then I saw

Josh, blowing his sax like a jazz pro. At his feet was a little metal bucket where passers-by could drop in coins.

Then I caught sight of the poster, mounted on a tripod.

I approached it, and was amazed to see a big, blown-up photograph of myself taken by a Scarborough newspaper to accompany a story about an operation I'd performed on a local celebrity.

The writing on the poster said: *"Due to laser operation by Mr Moghissi after my accident I am able again to play my saxophone."*

I had a nice, friendly chat with Josh and put some money in his bucket.

A little while later, I heard that the Scarborough Town Council had withdrawn Josh's street performer permit. Shop owners had complained that, because of his atrocious playing, there'd been a falling off of shoppers entering their stores.

The story was picked up by the 'Daily Mail' newspaper and published with a photograph of Josh, and the caption: "NO SAX PLEASE!"

A few weeks after this, I got a message from Josh asking if he could come and see me. My first thought was his condition must have worsened.

But, when he entered my office, he was bursting with vitality and, before I could recover from my surprise, he pressed fifteen pounds and fifty-eight pence in my hand.

It was one day's collection, he said, which he was donating to my Laser Trust charity. I knew he was in no position to donate to a charity, so I didn't want to take it. But he was insistent. It was important to him – a matter of pride.

So, I accepted it, and thanked him.

After he left, and closed the door, something broke inside me, and I felt like I was going to cry. But I stopped it. I didn't have time for it. There was too much to do.

I pulled myself together and got back to work.

17

THE MYSTERY OF FATHER O'NEILL

A 53-year-old priest, named Father O'Neill, had a chest deformity that was causing him pain. But, the day before he was due to arrive at my clinic, his General Practitioner phoned and advised me to cancel.

"Why?" I asked.

"He can't be in pain because he's not taking any medication."

"No medication?"

"That's right. He's faking."

Faking? My curiosity was aroused. Why would a 53-year-old Catholic priest lie about having a pain in his deformed chest? I could only assume that he didn't want to pay to have his chest corrected, so was trying to get it done on the National Health.

But why would a 53-year-old priest want to have his chest corrected? Surely not narcissism? If it were that, why had he left it so long?

I decided not to cancel his appointment.

Father O'Neill arrived, dressed in a long black cassock. He was a plump, pink-faced Irishman, a little below average height, with round, pale blue eyes, which rarely blinked.

We shook hands, and I asked him to sit down.

"I would prefer to stand," he said. "On account of when I sit, it pains me chest."

"I see."

I decided to dispense with talk about his medical history, and went straight to the examination.

Father O'Neill had a mild case of pectus excavatum (sunken chest), which wasn't noticeable unless he took his clothes off.

After he was back in his cassock, I expressed my view that he couldn't be in pain, and that an operation wouldn't do him any good.

To my surprise, he readily assented that he wasn't in pain. He said he needed the operation for cosmetic reasons.

"And, because I feel it would not be honorable to take another patient's place on the waiting list, I'm willing to pay for it."

"But why do you want this operation?" I asked. "What's the real reason?"

"'Tis God Almighty Himself who has directed me to it."

This took me aback. "God directed you to it?"

"Yes."

"Do you know why He directed you to it?"

"No, I can't say I do," replied the priest, his face adopting a holy look. "But Our Lord has reasons we mortals cannot know."

I thought for a moment, then I said: "No, I won't do your operation."

Now, it was the priest's turn to be taken aback.

"Why not?"

"Because God has directed me not to."

He went rigid. "I see."

Then he got up, gave me a nasty smile, shook his cassock, and walked out.

I still don't know why this 53-year-old Catholic priest wanted to have a cosmetic operation on his chest.

It's a mystery.

18

RIGHT OPERATION WRONG SIDE

I've trained many junior staff over the years. Some were highly competent, others so inept I couldn't help wondering how they'd ever qualified.

One trainee had a foot-high stack of diplomas – including the *Fellowship of the Royal College of Surgeons* – but couldn't make a straight incision. With a surgical knife in his hand, this man was dangerous!

But others, like Mario, were outstanding. While he was my trainee, Mario helped me set up a unit for open-heart surgery and, later, became a successful consultant surgeon in South America.

In 1981, after 10 years of planning and negotiations, I took charge of two new operating theatres. These were equipped with the latest technology, including a TV hook-up transmitting to the operating theatre the repeated biochemical profiling needed for cardiac operations.

These new theatres allowed me, and another consultant, to not only operate on more patients, but also to improve the teaching of our registrars.

My training method was to have the registrar perform the first steps of each operation. This meant doing a thoracotomy (opening the chest cavity), surveying the pathology, and devising and planning operative strategies.

Once this was done, the registrar would call me, and I'd join him – either to carry out the main part of the operation, or to have him perform it under my supervision.

It was in the spring of 1982, on a day when the sun was timidly beginning to revitalise nature, that I asked my trainee to start an operation on a lady with a tumour.

Thanks to biopsies and pre-operative investigations, we knew the tumour was of low-grade malignancy, and confined to the upper lobe of the right lung. All that was required was a limited lung resection.[33]

Sanjay, my trainee registrar, was a good surgeon, and had already done six months in our unit, so I intended to let him do the operation himself, with me assisting.

We'd discussed the programme thoroughly with the team that morning, so Sanjay was well-prepared.

Everything proceeded normally and, after about 40 minutes, I was called to the theatre.

[33] Removal of tissue.

I cleaned and disinfected my hands and forearms, put on a theatre gown and surgical gloves, and approached the operating table.

Immediately, I realised he'd opened the wrong side of the chest.

I turned to him, to hear his report.

He was looking bewildered.

"As you can see," he said, nervously. "I have opened the chest, and have done a preliminary assessment, but I cannot find any tumour! I cannot find any tumour anywhere!"

I knew what the problem was, but decided to check the X-rays first. But where were they? There were no X-rays on display. Had someone forgotten to put them up?

I finally located them, on a trolley with the patient's notes. I asked a nurse to put them up on the viewing box.

Sure enough, the tumour was in the right lung.

It was time to tell Sanjay.

"The reason you can't find it," I said, "is because you've opened the wrong side of the chest."

The young registrar looked as though he was going to faint. A nurse had to help him sit down.

Now I had a serious problem. How could we get out of this? I needed to think carefully. What were my options?

Option #1: Close the chest and start again on the other side.

– Not a good idea. The patient had signed her consent to one thoracotomy – not two. We'd be risking a lawsuit.

Option #2: Close the chest and, when the patient was fully conscious, explain the error, apologise profusely, and send her home. Then, when the wound was healed and she'd fully recovered, re-admit her, and do the operation properly.

– Would that work? No. The lady would be upset, even angry. She probably wouldn't agree to another operation. Not when the first one had been botched.

I studied the X-rays again, desperate to find an answer.

Then I saw it.

We could remove the tumour through the side that was open by going across the mid line, behind the top of the sternum. [34]

By extending the incision slightly over the chest, I could access the upper part of the right lung.

So, I carried out the lobectomy through the left chest. The only thing I had to do was change the position of the patient across the operating table, which was no problem.

My next tasks were to document the events as they'd occurred, and explain to the patient and her husband why she had a surgical wound on the left side of her chest, for

[34] Breast-bone.

removal of a tumour from her right lung.

Before I did this, though, I gave myself 20 minutes to listen to Bach's 'Chaconne for Solo Violin,' played by Yehudi Menuhin.

Then I went to the ward.

The patient was sitting up in bed, having a cup of tea with her relatives. I told her what had happened, and why.

She and her family listened attentively and, after I'd finished, said they understood.

"Mistakes happen," said the husband. "Don't worry. We won't make a song and dance about it."

When I told them I also had to report the case to hospital management, they offered to write a letter approving of my conduct, and expressing their appreciation of the frank way they'd been told about the mishap.

I was greatly relieved. My registrar and I had dodged a bullet.

And I resolved to think no more about it.

But my mind kept returning to the incident. Why? It kept bothering me, like I had a stone in my shoe.

Then, later that day, it hit me. The urgent need to find a solution to my registrar's mistake had revealed a way to remove two or more secondary tumours from both lungs using only one incision. Eureka!

(Later, I developed a method, using a laser, to remove secondary tumours in both lungs in just one operation. Were it not for my registrar's mistake, I never would have seen it.)

As for the Indian registrar, it was my duty, as his teacher, to scold him. He'd made a grave mistake.

I called him to my office.

When he was standing before me, I said: "Sanjay, you must never – ever – start an incision before examining the X-rays first!"

"Yes sir, I know. I'm sorry," he said, quivering with emotion. "It will never happen again, I promise."

"It better not!"

I let him stew for a moment, then told him that, however, due to his previous good performance – and a possible intervention by Shiva[35] – no action would be taken, and the incident would not go down on his record.

A few months later, after Sanjay had left our hospital, I received a package from him.

I opened it, and unwrapped a beautifully carved wooden statue of the Hindu god Saraswati.[36]

I still have it.

[35] Shiva is supreme among Indian deities. He protects and transforms the universe.
[36] Saraswati – goddess of knowledge, art, and wisdom.

19

DAVID

Whenever I hear the name David, my mind goes back to a side ward in a hospital in North-West England where, one autumn evening, a man I loved spoke his last dying words.

From humble beginnings, David worked his way up the ladder of surgical training to become a consultant cardiothoracic surgeon – a hard path requiring a sustained uphill effort.

He was one of my best trainees and I was privileged to be a kind of father figure to him.

As I write this, it seems like only a day or two since he first knocked on my door.

"Come in!" I called.

The door opened, and a slim, well-dressed young man came in. I recognised him straightaway as the doctor we'd appointed as my new registrar.

Before I opened my mouth, he said: "I'm here to say I'm ready to start work on Monday."

"But what about your holidays? Don't you have holiday time left?"

He dismissed this with a shake of his head. "Yes, but I want to get started. All I need is the week-end to sort things out, and I can be back Sunday night to start work on Monday."

This reminded me of my first appointment as a house surgeon at Edgware Hospital, when I went in at the weekend before I was due to start work, to become acquainted with the job.

"Well, I wasn't expecting you," I said, "but now you're here, sit down and I'll explain how we do things."

For the next hour, we talked about the working structure of the department, about medical staffing, and about our ongoing research.

After that, I showed him around the wards.

By the time we finished, it was 7 o'clock.

It was Friday and, on Fridays, I usually had dinner at the hospital because that was the day when Edwina, our chef, made delicious fish and chips with mushy peas.

"Do you have plans for dinner?" I asked David. "I'm going to have fish and chips in the canteen. Would you like to join me, or would you rather go home?"

"I'd be happy to join you, boss. Fish and chips ought to be good in Hull."

So, we went to the canteen, queued for our dinner with our trays, and I learned, among other things, that he was married, and that his wife, a solicitor, worked in another city.

For the year of his training, David would be resident at the hospital.

Monday morning was soon upon us, and I discovered my new registrar, nicely attired, waiting for me in the ward.

"What are you doing here at this hour?" I said.

"Well, you told me at the interview that, if I wanted to be trained by you, I should be in the ward half an hour before you are, and not leave till you've gone." He grinned at me. "So, here I am!"

He was right. At David's interview, I'd said: 'If a trainee wants to be trained by me, he should be in the ward before I start in the morning, and should not leave the hospital before I do in the evening.'

This had vexed the chairman of the appointments committee and, after David had left the room, he hauled me over the coals for saying it.

The reason was a new ruling by the Department of Health imposing shorter working hours, and more weekends off, for junior staff.

I'd been very vocal on this issue, telling various organisations I didn't believe a person could be trained properly in cardiothoracic surgery if the new rules came into effect.

"But," I said to David, "I'm going to Scarborough to do a clinic, and won't be back till 4 o'clock."

"Can I come with you?"

"Wouldn't you rather stay here and see what's going on in the wards?"

"I'd rather come with you."

"All right," I said. "If that's what you want, let's go."

As we drove to Scarborough in my car, we talked about the new work regulations. These didn't impress David. He said he wasn't coming to my department to learn guidelines but to be trained in cardiothoracic surgery. He welcomed the extra work because of the knowledge he would gain from it.

This pleased me very much.

"If you want to learn," I said, "you have to shadow me. Emergencies in thoracic surgery happen at unexpected times. It's no good being on emergency call only once every three days. You have to be around more than that. The more you're around, the more you see, and the quicker you gain experience."

His reply was, "I'll be there."

And he was true to his word.

Our car journey also allowed me to test his knowledge. I discovered that he knew a lot about the cardiac side of the discipline, and had a good theoretical knowledge of thoracic surgery. What he lacked was practical experience – which was why, of course, he was in a training post.

Like many young surgeons, David was fascinated by cardiac surgery. The first time you see an open-heart operation, with all the sophisticated monitoring devices, and the amazing cardio-pulmonary by-pass machine, which circulates blood outside the body, it's awe-inspiring.

And then there's the drama of stopping the heart, which we have to do in order to carry out intra-cardiac operations.

Then, after the cardiac incision is closed, there's the drama of re-starting the heart.

The heart is electrically shocked to stimulate contraction. The observer is on tenterhooks. "Will the heart start or not?" Then it beats – very slowly – then picks up speed, like a steam engine puffing out of a railway station.

From day one, David followed me, and made notes of my every move. He was a loyal and reliable assistant, and was also popular with the nurses and the junior staff.

That year, one of my Senior House Officers, who was good at practical work, was having problems getting through his final examinations – the fearsome *Fellowship of the Royal College of Surgeons.*

David, who already had this qualification, spent time with him, passing on 'tricks of the trade,' such as how to deal with questions, and how to dress for the viva.[37]

I'm pretty sure that the house officer's subsequent passing of the exam was, in part, due to David's coaching.

David was a great help with my research projects, and numerous publications, and I also found in him someone with a God-given talent for presenting medical research. So, I took him with me to several conferences.

Our most outstanding presentations were probably at the *European Association for Cardio-Thoracic Surgery* in London, and two papers we gave at the *European Respiratory Society* in Glasgow and Florence.

For the London meeting, I secured sponsorship for my research team to attend not only the meeting, but also the dinner afterwards. The dinner was held at the Guildhall, after which we were blasted by a rousing march played by the Band of the Grenadier Guards!

When I asked David to present our medical laser research in Florence, he was willing but anxious. This was the first time the European Respiratory Society had devoted an entire session to lasers – and the first time David had presented a paper abroad.

To nail down the accuracy of the data, and ensure David

[37] Oral examination, when the student demonstrates his ability to verbally defend his thesis and participate in academic discussion.

could cover it all in the allotted time, we did three rehearsals.

What worried him most was the discussion afterwards.

I passed on what I'd been told by one of my mentors: 'When you're presenting a paper based on your research, you don't need to be intimidated by audience members more senior and experienced than yourself. No one has more knowledge about your work than you do. Say what you know, and don't be drawn into guesswork.'

In the event, his presentation was masterful, and he handled the questions brilliantly.

When it was over, he was elated. He kept saying: "Boss, I was fine with it, really fine with it! I even enjoyed it! And it was because I was completely confident that no one – except you – knew more about the subject than I did!"

It gave us both a lot of pleasure.

To celebrate, I arranged a dinner party, and invited various friends, including a former assistant of mine from Rome – a witty conversationalist, with very good English, named Nikola.

Nikola was a welcome guest at my parties, to which he brought a touch of Roman joviality and exuberance. He and David got on like a house on fire.

By the time his year in my department had ended, David had made real progress in clinical and laboratory research, and also in the practice of thoracic surgery. And he'd put together some first-rate research papers, as well.

For me, personally, he was a warm, enthusiastic companion, who stimulated me intellectually.

One day he said to me: "What drives you, boss? What makes you work so hard?"

I didn't think I was working so hard, but I replied by saying: "Have you ever come across the poet Longfellow?"

"No."

"Well, many years ago, when I was working as a registrar, and doing research, and studying for the FRCS, I was inspired by some lines from one of his poems."

The heights by great men reached and kept
Were not attained by sudden flight,
But, they while their companions slept,
Were toiling upward in the night.[38]

"I asked a calligrapher to write it in black and gold," I said. "And I put it in front of me, on my desk."

He took this seriously and adopted these lines for himself.

A few years after David left Hull, he became a consultant in cardiothoracic surgery at the Victoria Hospital, in Blackpool. I knew the town well, having worked there

[38] From 'The Ladder of St. Augustine.'

when the Cardiothoracic Surgery Department was still in its infancy.

During my time there, it was a happy place with two very good consultant thoracic surgeons.

I imagined David walking down the same corridors I'd walked down, although, back then, my walk as a registrar was a lot shakier than his would be as a consultant!

David now had a demanding job, but that didn't stop him pursuing the research he was still doing jointly with me. And, at the same time, he also formulated a teaching programme for cardiac surgery.

I was extremely proud of him. He was making a name for himself, both as a surgeon and as an organiser, and was elevating the reputation and status of his medical centre. The wind was in his sails, and his future plans were bold and exciting.

Then I received a phone call.

"Boss, I think I'm in trouble."

He'd noticed an involuntary movement in one of his arms, and had had it investigated.

He had a brain tumour.

Fortunately, it didn't affect his intellect, or his competency as a surgeon – but he needed treatment.

We were in the middle of a number of projects, including

a new chapter for the second edition of *'Moghissi's Essentials of Thoracic and Cardiac Surgery.'*

"I'll try to finish the chapter," he said.

"Don't worry about that now," I said. "Just get better. And if I can do anything, let me know."

But he finished the chapter, and the book wasn't delayed because of him. It was delayed by two other contributors, who were both in perfect health!

David's tumour was aggressive, so his treatment was surgery, chemotherapy, and radiation. He bore it all with fortitude and, afterwards, continued to be optimistic.

Soon after he was back on his feet, my book came out and David and his wife came to the publication party.

But, in September, the tumour returned. This was a heavy blow. By now, he had a son, aged six, and a baby daughter.

Knowing he was unlikely to survive, David began putting his affairs in order – all the while maintaining a positive attitude.

When I visited him at his home, he was in good spirits. He talked about the teaching project he'd started at the hospital, and was full of plans for the future.

We were still able to laugh and joke.

A month later, in October, I got a call saying David had been hospitalised and was receiving terminal care.

This was a shock.

He wanted me to come and see him, so I cancelled all my appointments, and drove to Blackpool with my friend, Kate, who knew both David and his wife.

It took us over two hours to get there.

The sun – a swollen red ball – slowly sank below the tree line. There was a chill in the air. Summer was definitely over.

We walked into the hospital, which was bigger and more impressive than when I'd last seen it – but it still felt familiar. For some moments, I was caught in a mist – seeing the tall figure of my old chief, with his elegant mannerisms and his charming Aberdonian accent, doing his ward rounds, followed by his registrar (me), and Miss Featherstone, the ward sister, a little woman, kind and caring, who walked with a limp, and was known for her no-nonsense principles.

"No time for this!" I said to myself.

I found David's wife sitting calmly, but her eyes showed unmistakeable signs of trauma. I'd seen this before on the faces of women with small children on the point of being widowed. They bleed inside but produce no tears. Their hearts are broken, but they're being strong for the children.

What can you say to such a person when you see her, stiff with pain, trying to smile because you've come a long way to see her husband?

I was told David was fully conscious of what was happening, and had asked for his drugs to be suspended until after he'd seen me. I was the last person, other that his wife, he was going to speak to.

I entered his room, which was in semi darkness – probably because he had photophobia. In a surprisingly strong voice, he asked me to sit down and, in spite of the tubes and drips, rolled himself to the edge of the bed.

Then he talked about his life.

He said how wretched it was to know he wouldn't see his children grow up. Then he spoke about his wife and other members of his family. He wanted to tell me secrets – things he'd previously kept to himself. This was deeply flattering, but also a responsibility.

But the sadness faded when we began to recall past incidents. And, for over three quarters of an hour, we reminisced about things we'd done together, including many funny moments. We even talked about our first fish and chips, and chuckled about the mushy peas which, on that occasion, had been cold.

It didn't feel like this was the last time I was going to see him.

Then the mood changed.

"I'm glad you could come," he said, and fell silent.

He couldn't speak anymore.

Then came a wave of unbearable sorrow. I moved on to his bed, and held his head on my chest to comfort him – and myself.

The last words he whispered to me were: "Boss, I want out. When you leave, could you call the nurse to restart my drugs?"

I did what he asked and, after that, my mind went blank.

The next thing I knew I was in a car, driven by my friend Kate, on the M62 motorway.

David died on 25th of October, 2003. In recognition of his work, a memorial symposium in his name was established by the Lancashire Cardiac Centre.

I remain angry at his death, and mourn him still.

20

HAZEL'S HONEYMOON

In 1987, a letter arrived from a colleague I'd met at a medical conference who had a friend in Malta, named Mr. Sabatini.

Mr. Sabatini had lung cancer.

Because of the extent of the tumour, he needed an operation to remove the affected lung,[39] followed by chemotherapy and radiotherapy. But, before saying goodbye to one of his lungs, Mr. Sabatini wanted a second opinion.

Could he come to Britain to see me?

Before agreeing to this, I needed to get some background history, and see his medical notes.

A week later, I got the information, including the latest X-rays and, after examining them carefully, came to the conclusion that he didn't have cancer at all. It looked to me like a chronic lung abscess.

If I was right, he needed an operation entailing the loss of no more than an upper portion of his left lung.

The day after giving my opinion, I had a surprising

[39] Pneumonectomy.

message saying Mr. Sabatini had just landed in London and wanted to come straight up to Yorkshire and see me.

He must have left for the airport as soon as he got my message!

And when he arrived with his wife, they were carrying so many bags of chocolates, sweetmeats, and local Maltese wines, that they barely got through the door!

I carried out a clinical examination and, after more tests, confirmed he had a lung abscess (a pool of pus surrounded by a membrane).

Three days later, I did the operation with no more than a 25% loss to the left lung.

Ten days after that, he was fully recovered and ready to return to Malta.

Mr. Sabatini – who worked in the tourist industry, and owned holiday apartments – came to my office to say goodbye.

"I invite you to Malta," he said, "to have one of my apartments for your holidays for as long as you wish. Just let me know a couple of weeks beforehand, and I will see that you have a good time. I also have motor boats, and can put one of them at your disposal for as long as you like to stay in Malta."

I thanked him for his kind offer, and told him I would arrange for him to be followed up in Malta. But he shook his head. No. He didn't trust the Maltese doctors. He would come to England to see me for his follow-ups.

So, this is what he did. He came in for check-ups: two months, then six months, and then a year after the operation. Finally, as all was well, I discharged him from the clinic.

Two years later, while on a trip to the UK, he dropped in to see me. Again, he showered me with presents – including a beautifully made, silver and wood, miniature replica of the Santa Maria galleon. And, again, he begged me to accept his invitation to have a holiday in one of his beach-front apartments.

As fate would have it, I never saw Mr. Sabatini again. However, I did have news of him from a patient of mine named Hazel – a girl I first met when she was nine years old.

Hazel was a lovely child with blue eyes, black hair, and a complexion like a Victorian porcelain doll. Unfortunately, she had a hole in her heart,[40] together with a narrowing of the pulmonary artery valve.[41]

During my training in London, I'd been instructed in all aspects of pediatric cardiothoracic operations and, by the time Hazel was referred to me, I was practiced in repairing the type of congenital defect she suffered from.

[40] Ventricular septal defect.
[41] Pulmonary stenosis.

Our 8-bed children's ward, which served an area from Hull to as far north as Whitby, had intensive care services, and a well-trained team for pediatric cardiac surgery.

Our small children's ward, which I'd created in a building separate from the main hospital, was the jewel in the crown of our cardiothoracic unit. Its hand-picked nursing team was second to none. In fact, one could easily have imagined it being part of a dedicated children's hospital.

We had already repaired heart defects in 30 children without complications, or a single fatality.

Using the heart-lung machine,[42] I successfully carried out an operation to correct Hazel's hole-in-the-heart.

For 48 hours after the operation, our devoted team of intensive care nurses looked after her. Then, she was moved to the children's ward.

Ten days later, she was discharged.

Several months after her operation, Hazel's heart rhythm became irregular. This was because of a heart block, due to scarring. She needed a Heart Pacemaker.

Like most of the children I'd operated on, she was very much at home in the unit, treating me and the nursing staff like members of the family.

[42] Cardio-pulmonary bypass.

Typically, Hazel would enter the outpatients' clinic with her mum and run towards me full of excitement. She'd stand beside my chair and show me drawings she'd done and tell me about her school activities.

Time passed and, eventually, she became an attractive 21-year-old.

In 1989, while visiting me in Outpatients, she introduced me to her fiancé.

"When are you going to be married?" I asked.

"Soon. In a couple of months."

"Are you having a big wedding and a honeymoon?"

"Oh no, we can't afford that. We'll have a small wedding – just for the family." She smiled, with a lovely expression, at her fiancé who was a little uncomfortable being in the clinic. "And my auntie's giving us some money for a weekend in Scarborough."

'Hm. Not much of a honeymoon,' I thought.

"We've put down a deposit on a small flat," she continued, "and we need every penny of our savings to fix it up. Our dads are going to help us with the painting and decorating."

Without warning, something struck my hypothalamus (the area in the brain regulating emotive functions.)

I knew what I had to do.

While Hazel was getting ready to be examined in the next

room, I asked my secretary to find me Mr. Sabatini's phone number. Then I went to talk to Hazel's fiancé – a pleasant, honest young man, who was looking forward to setting up home with his sweetheart.

Once her examination was over, I asked Hazel and her boyfriend to wait, and went into my office to make a phone call.

"Good morning Mr. Sabatini, this is M…"

Before I could finish my sentence, he said: "Aha! At last you will accept my invitation! When are you coming to Malta?"

"Well, actually, I'm not. I'm calling to ask you a favour."

"But of course – anything."

"Could your invitation be passed on to a young patient of mine who's getting married but can't afford a honeymoon?"

"Absolutely!"

I returned to the examination room, sat down and said: "Well, Hazel, first of all, I'm pleased with your progress, and can tell you that, as far as your heart's concerned, there's no reason why you shouldn't have children. Secondly, I was wondering if you'd like to have a week in Malta for your honeymoon?"

Hazel looked at her fiancé, then turned to me. "I don't expect to have a family for quite a few years yet. And, as for a honeymoon, we can't afford it. All the money we've saved has to go on the flat."

"Don't worry," I said. "The honeymoon is free."

Hazel and her fiancé looked at me in confusion, so I explained about Mr. Sabatini. All they needed to do was give the date to my secretary and she'd take care of their accommodation and their travel expenses.

At that time, I booked my flights through a travel agency whose manager was also one of my patients. When my secretary rang, asking for two tickets to Malta, his response was:

"At last he (that is me) is taking a holiday!"

When she said the flights were for a young couple, and told him the story, the manager declared it would be his pleasure to arrange two free return flights.

His only condition was that his gift be anonymous.

So, Mr. Sabatini provided the bride and groom's holiday flat, the major part of their travel was covered by the travel agency, and a third individual – as a wedding present – came up with some spending money.

Hazel and her bridegroom went on their honeymoon, and had a wonderful time. I know this because I got a postcard from her almost every day.

I feel privileged to have been a part of Hazel's life, whose heart I'd repaired as a child, and who I watched grow into a fine young woman. The feelings of reward and satisfaction this gave me are beyond my powers of description.

21

MR JACK BRADLEY

When I became the city of Hull's consultant cardiothoracic surgeon, it was on condition that I conduct a weekly clinic in Scarborough. I didn't mind this. Scarborough is a charming seaside town, famous for its spectacular bay and its theatre – home to the playwright, Alan Ayckbourn.

My clinic took place on Monday mornings between 9.30 and 1.30 pm. After this, I grabbed a snack lunch and drove to my consulting room, which I rented from the town council in an imposing edifice known as 'The Lodge.'

The Lodge was a beautiful building, dating from the 1830's, specifically furnished as private consulting rooms for doctors.

One of its major assets was a concierge, named Mary, who also acted as a receptionist.

Mary was a good-natured, well-spoken, grey-haired lady of about 65, who offered patients tea or coffee, and would chat with them if the consultant was late.

One sunny afternoon in 1983, I saw a referral, Jack Bradley, who'd been diagnosed with cancer of the oesophagus. He entered my consulting room wearing a flea-bitten flat cap, a crumpled open-necked shirt, no tie, a shapeless jacket, and trousers that looked like they'd never seen a hot iron.

What struck me as odd was that he wasn't local. He'd come all the way to Scarborough from a village outside Leeds. Why had his GP referred him to me? There was a perfectly good oesophageal surgeon in Leeds, and another one in nearby Bradford.

After the usual pleasantries, I got down to business.

"Now, sir, tell me what the problem is."

He gave me a startled look, then said: "They told me I 'ad cancer in me goollet." (That's gullet if you haven't guessed.)

I asked him when the trouble started.

He told me – at some length – and when he was finished, he fixed me with his eyes and said: "Not a soul in Leeds 'as ever called me 'sir.'"

I didn't know how to respond to this.

"Not a soul 'as ever called me 'sir,'" he repeated.

"I did it as a mark of respect."

"Aye," he grunted, and looked at the floor.

I consulted his case records, and then examined him.

As luck would have it, his cancer could be treated with surgical resection and reconstruction.

When I told him this, I also said I could perform the

operation, under the NHS, at my hospital in Hull.

"Nay, nay. I don't want the NHS," he said, firmly. "I want to pay."

"You want to pay? Why?"

"I want the best."

"But I'll be doing the operation whether you pay or not."

"I don't care. I want the best. And I don't want me operation done by one o' them foreigners!"

"But I'm a foreigner," I said.

"I don't care," he said. "You called me 'sir.'"

A few weeks later, Mr Bradley came to Hull, had his operation (privately) and, so far as I know, wasn't troubled by cancer again.

22

A HOME VISIT

In the 1970s and 1980s, it wasn't uncommon for consultants to make home visits at the request of General Practitioners.

Domiciliary visits, as they were called, were good for patients who needed an urgent consultation. And, when the GP wasn't sure if the patient should go to hospital or not, a home visit would sort things out.

Compared with physicians, surgeons didn't do many home visits, and I did even less because of my full operating schedule. But I did manage to carry out about one every two weeks – usually for GPs I knew I could trust not to waste my time.

One Wednesday morning, in the midst of an operation, I got an urgent message to call a GP friend of mine named Mike.

As soon as the operation was over, I called him, and heard about a 38-year-old female named Mrs Beverly who, early that morning had brought up, what Mike called, a cup full of bright, red blood.[43]

[43] Haemoptysis.

"Don't you think she'd better come in? I said.

"She says she can't. She has to sleep."

"Does she work at night?"

"Part of the night, yes."

"Well, the trouble is I'm busy all day. The soonest I could see her would be this evening."

"That would be fine. I'll tell her. Thanks."

When I'd finished my operating list, and checked on my patients, it was 7.30pm – the time my medical researchers started work. I asked one of them, Kate, if she wouldn't mind coming with me on a home visit, so she could give me a research report in the car.

She agreed, and we drove out of the hospital.

I had the address of Mrs Beverly, and an elementary roadmap of how to get there, prepared by my secretary. I passed the paper to Kate who glanced at it and smiled.

"I don't need a map for this. I've known this place all my life."

'Aren't I lucky to have a native with me?' I thought.

Mrs Beverly lived in an apartment in a worn-out tower block. The block's entrance was a dark alley. The streetlight was out, and the light above the block's entrance had been shattered.

When we entered the lobby, there was a strong smell of urine.

Mrs Beverly lived on the 7th floor. Mercifully, both lifts were working.

We reached the 7th floor, and stepped out into a dark corridor with three doors. We had the number, but there weren't any numbers on the doors. Concentrating our vision, we made out some hard-to-read numbers scratched on the walls.

At last, we'd found it.

I pressed the bell and, after a couple of seconds, there was a distant chiming. There was a delay on the bell. Even the bell was worn out!

Finally, a woman opened the door.

She led us into the sitting room, then left us to go into another room. A few minutes later, a man came out of this room and, without saying a word, left the flat.

It wasn't hard to imagine what Mrs Beverly's night work was, and why she needed to sleep during the day.

A few moments later, she returned to the sitting room.

Mrs Beverly was thin, refined looking, well-dressed, with good manners. I doubt if anyone would have guessed her occupation.

She told me she had a bad cough, and sputum, and that she'd been spitting blood.

On examination, I became concerned about her chest,

and thought she should be admitted in case she had a larger bleeding. This could be dangerous. She didn't like the idea, but agreed.

So, I arranged for an ambulance, and then phoned the on-call registrar to let him know of the admission, and to give him her history.

This turned out to be timely because, soon after her arrival at the hospital, she did have a larger bleeding, which we were able to stop.

After a full investigation, she needed only a small operation to cauterise the bleeding point. I did this using a laser I'd recently acquired. I also found a tumour (benign), which had caused a small lung abscess.

The tumour and abscess were treated with my new laser, avoiding the need for a major operation.

While at the hospital, she was visited by her daughter – a good-looking university student, studying languages, and hoping to work as a teacher in France.

The mother was working to support her daughter.

"I want my daughter to have better opportunities than I had," she told me one evening. She said her daughter didn't know about her profession. She thought she earned her money by sewing and dress making, which she also did.

It saddened me to think that, in an advanced country

like ours, good people like Mrs Beverly have to resort to prostitution in order to educate their children.

Mrs Beverly left the hospital much healthier than when she came in, and promised to give up smoking.

At the first outpatients' clinic, she handed me a small package wrapped in fancy paper, which had a sticker on it saying: *Harvey Nichols.*[44]

The package contained two elegant pocket handkerchiefs, which nicely matched some of my ties.

But I didn't want to accept them.

"No, please," she said. "Take them. As a token of my appreciation. Not only for helping me, but also for praising me to my daughter."

I had told her daughter she should be proud of her mother, who I regarded as a person of high moral integrity.

"All right," I said, accepting the handkerchiefs. "Thank you."

[44] An up-market London department store.

23

DINOSAURS IN DOG COLLARS

I first met Jackie in 1974. She was 8 years old – a shy, well-looked-after, dark-haired little thing with a shining smile.

She was trying not to cough but, when she couldn't resist the 'tickle' any longer, a little burst of coughing erupted, followed by uneven, rattled breathing.

As her mother began to give me her clinical history, I guessed that the girl had *bronchiectasis* – a condition in which the air conducting tubes of the lungs (the bronchial tree) are dilated.

In bronchiectasis, the swollen bronchial tubes secrete an increased production of sputum, so a large amount of 'phlegm' collects in the lungs. Colonisation by infective microorganisms then creates pools of pus that spread through the pulmonary tissues, causing chest infections and damage to lung tissue.

In the 19th century, before the discovery of antibiotics, many bronchiectasis sufferers – usually children and young adults – died of pneumonia, or cardio-respiratory failure.

Once I'd examined Jackie, I arranged for her to

have a bronchoscopy,[45] and various X-rays, including a bronchography – which delivers an outline of the interior of the bronchial tree using a fluid that is radio-opaque. These investigations were needed to exclude other pathologies, such as endo-bronchial tumours, or the presence of foreign bodies inhaled accidentally.

To undergo these tests, Jackie was admitted to Castle Hill Hospital, some 50 miles from her home. This meant her mother had to come to the hospital and stay in the ward with her.

The tests confirmed that Jackie had extensive damage in the lower part of both her lungs.

For the record, I should mention that I'd established an 8-bed children's ward, staffed by very competent paediatric nurses, headed by a Sister trained at Great Ormond Street Children's Hospital, in London.

I'd also made provision for the parents to stay in the ward with their children.

From its launch at the beginning of 1972, this ward, with its staff, was a great asset to my department – and I fought tooth and nail to keep it open.

After the tests were completed, it was clear that Jackie

[45] Examination of the interior of the airway.

needed two separate operations to remove the lower half of each lung, both of them so diseased that they'd ceased to function.

Before embarking on surgery, I wanted Jackie to undergo a programme of physiotherapy, supplemented by a regime of bronchial disinfection.

I first became aware of bronchial disinfection when I was a medical student in Switzerland in the early 1950s.

As a young intern, I used to accompany my chief to the tuberculosis sanatoria in Montana, in the Swiss Alps, to assist him with operations. Here, I was introduced to bronchial lavage.

Bronchial lavage entails injecting sterile saline solution, mixed with antibiotics, or an aqueous disinfectant solution, into the bronchial tubes. The fluid mixes with the infected secretions and is then removed by suction.

When I became a consultant, after a pilot study, I started bronchial lavage on patients with chronic broncho-pulmonary sepsis, using a diluted disinfectant. I found this effective in reducing the frequency of chest infections, and we were able to cut admissions to the hospital by at least 50%.

Also, in patients with pathogens resistant to antibiotics, six weekly sessions of bronchial lavage eliminated the organisms, so surgery could take place with the patient free from infection.

Jackie had received frequent courses of antibiotics before her referral to my clinic, so her sputum contained microbial and fungal organisms resistant to antibiotics.

We carried out bronchial lavage with a disinfectant every two months for a year. This eliminated the fungal organisms – and, naturally, we avoided repeat prescriptions of the antibiotics to which the microbes had become resistant.

Finally, little Jackie was ready to submit to the first operation – a left lower lobectomy.[46]

This was successfully carried out.

I've always been tremendously impressed by children who undergo a major chest operation. They handle the pain and psychological suffering with great courage. Despite this, before the operation, I was worried that the two weeks Jackie needed to be in hospital for preoperative preparations, surgery and post-operative recovery, might prove traumatic because she was a very sensitive little girl.

As it turned out, I was wrong. Jackie loved being with us, and her mum was able to be there with her most of the time.

I would call into the children's ward twice a day, and at odd times at night, to see the ward nurses looking after the children and giving them the family atmosphere that is an

[46] Removal of the lower part of the left lung.

essential part of their care.

When Jackie was discharged, she needed to be followed up to monitor the progress of the lung on the operated side, and to prevent infection of the unoperated lung.

She was seen regularly at the Scarborough outpatients' clinic and, every few months, she came to Castle Hill for bronchial lavage.

This regime continued for two years before the operation for the right lower lobectomy was scheduled. The preparations for this were easier than for the first operation because, for Jackie, the ward was a home-from-home.

I've often felt that, for a surgeon, performing an operation is rather like a concert violinist playing a concerto in a concert hall. No matter how many times one has played a concerto (or performed an operation), there is always a feeling of fear and excitement, before the start.

Making the skin incision to expose the area needing surgery is like the opening introduction by the orchestra before the solo part begins. And, no matter how expert the violinist – or surgeon – may be, something unexpected can always happen. Strings can break.

But, I'm happy to say, no strings broke during Jackie's second operation, which was completed without complications.

Follow-ups as an outpatient were arranged to monitor her progress, and I agreed to carry out domiciliary visits, to reduce the number of Jackie's absences from school. Doing this was no hardship because their home was on the way to Scarborough Hospital where, every fortnight, I travelled to do endoscopies.[47]

In fact, the visits were most enjoyable. I would examine and assess Jackie's progress, and then have tea with homemade cakes, and enjoy the warmth of her family.

One Monday morning, near midday, when I was about to end my clinic, I had a call from Jackie's mum, asking if I could call in on my way back to Hull.

"Is anything wrong?"

"Nay, she just wants your opinion on summat."

At about 3.30, I arrived at the cottage, wondering what it was all about.

The reason was revealed when I was introduced to a tall, shy young man named Tom.

Jackie's mother took me into the kitchen.

"Tom and Jackie 'ave been seeing each other," she whispered. "And now they're talking about gettin' married. We need your opinion of him."

[47] Examining the interior of the body using an endoscope or flexible tube with a relay lens connected to a screen.

"My opinion?" I was amazed.

"Yes. Jackie looks on you as her 'clever uncle.' And my husband wants your advice on it too."

Jackie's father, Ivon, was a shepherd – a strong man who didn't talk much.

I said I'd do my best to discreetly make an assessment of Jackie's intended.

We returned to the parlour.

Jackie's beau, Tom – a young farmer – although shy, struck me as both decent and intelligent. He was very attentive to Jackie and – importantly for her condition – he didn't smoke.

I told the parents I thought they'd make a good match.

It wasn't long before the invitation for the wedding arrived. It was to be a church wedding followed by a reception for the family and friends in the pub where Jackie worked.

Such a nice, simple way of getting married, I thought.

At the reception, there was no question of following the formality of usual weddings. We all sat at the pub tables, and the drinks were courtesy of the pub's landlord.

Being regarded as a member of the family, my wife and I were seated at Jackie's parents' table. Before we started lunch, Ivon asked if I could do him a favour.

"I never stood up to talk in front of folks before," he said, quietly. "Can you gie us a speech instead o' me?"

I was really surprised. "Are you sure?"

"Aye."

This was such a great compliment that I had to do it. But what on earth would I say? I couldn't very well give a speech about her hospital case history.

So, I asked Ivon for any funny incidents from her childhood – a mischievous prank at school perhaps? But he told me he didn't know about any of that because he was always away with his flocks. I could identify because, as a surgeon, I wasn't home much either – I was away with my flocks too (my patients.)

Ivon pointed me to Margaret, his wife, who was a lot more helpful.

Far too quickly, the time came for the father of the bride to make a speech.

Ivon, looking very uncomfortable, stood up and said: "Mr M. will say a few words for me."

Jackie was wearing a white wedding gown, and there were little girls in pretty dresses running around, as I stood up and began to speak about the loving personality of the brave young girl I'd first met when she was eight years-old.

Without referring much to her condition, I recalled how, when she saw me in the outpatients' clinic, she would give me a kiss on the cheek, and tell me about school and what she'd done that day. And I spoke about how rewarding it was to watch her grow up, and to see her blossom into a beautiful young bride.

I think I got away with my impromptu speech, the wedding went well, and Jackie and her husband wrote me a lovely letter afterwards.

I still have it, together with a photo of the wedding.

Days, weeks, and months passed as I carried on with follow-ups on Jackie, and the occasional bronchial lavage.

A couple of years later, Jackie became pregnant and gave birth to a healthy boy. A few years after that, there was a second pregnancy, and another boy was born.

Several weeks after the birth of her second son, I had a call from her, telling me that she and her husband wanted me to be the godfather to their second boy, Sam.

I was very flattered.

"Are you sure about this?" I asked.

"Absolutely sure."

"Well, then I'll be more than pleased. Just let me know a couple of weeks beforehand."

A few weeks passed, and I had a call from a Reverend Gerald Garnet, of Hoxton Village Church.

"Doctor, Jackie and her husband have asked me to christen their son and have named you as the godfather. I expect they have contacted you?"

"Yes, indeed they have, and I'm pleased to accept."

"How long have you known Jackie and her husband?"

"Almost 20 years."

"I assume you are baptised within the Church of England?"

"No," I replied. "I'm not of the Christian faith. I'm a Bahá'í."

There was a puzzled pause.

"I've never heard of this religion. What is it? What do you believe in?"

"Bahá'í's believe in the oneness of mankind, the eradication of prejudice, the equality of men and women..."

"But you're not a Christian," he interrupted. "Are you?"

"No, I'm not."

"So, you cannot be godfather to a child who was baptised in my Church."

"I wonder what Jesus would have said about that?"

"I have no idea," he replied. "I'm not Jesus."

After this, I had a call from Jackie, who was very distressed.

"Please don't be upset," I said. "It's not the end of the world. The priest is simply acting according to the rules of the Church of England. I'm afraid there's nothing we can do about it."

I find it regrettable that, in the turbulent world we live in, so many churches are intolerant. The clergy worry about people growing away from them, yet they refuse to accommodate their needs.

They're dinosaurs in dog collars.

24

HARRY

One bright Saturday, in the summer of 1989, I'd parked my car near Hull City Centre, and was walking to the City Hall with Alex, my wife, to buy tickets for a concert.

Alex, noticing a man running across the road towards us, tugged at my sleeve.

I turned and saw an excited-looking man, with flapping hair, coming straight at us, pulling off his jacket and his shirt.

Something about him looked familiar, but I didn't know who he was.

"It's me, Mr. M!" he yelled. "Don't you recognise me?"

He dumped his shirt and jacket on the pavement, and lifted his undershirt. "Fifteen years ago, remember?"

He came up close, and displayed his naked chest. Passers-by stopped to look. We began to feel embarrassed.

"You cut me ches'!" the man cried. "It was all excavatin'!"

There was, indeed, a scar typical of an incision for a repair of a chest deformity.

"Champion, in't it?" said the man, proudly.

I looked at him. He was smiling from ear to ear.

"Ta for that!" he said.

Then his wife, from the other side of the road, yelled out: "Harry! *Harry!* You comin' back or wot!?"

With a big grin, the man picked up his clothes and ran off, back to his wife.

"Who was that?" asked my better half.

"Harry," I said.

25

SO, YOU WANT TO BE A UROLOGIST?

At 10.30 p.m., after a long day's work, I decided to sit down, put my feet up, and watch *Question Time* on BBC1.

I turned on the TV just at the moment when its loud, jangling signature tune signalled the arrival of David Dimbleby, the show's host.

The first question concerned Muslim nurses who were demanding to wear the hijab and niquab on duty. This garment covers the entire body from head to toe, so only the eyes are seen.

The question was: 'Would the members of the panel like to be nursed by someone wearing a head-to-toe hijab with niquab?'

The responses from the panellists were cautiously worded so as not to upset the Muslim community. However, reading between the lines, it was clear that no-one wanted to be treated by a nurse wearing a black, beekeeper's outfit.

Then Mr. Dimbleby turned to ask members of the audience for their views.

Some said people should be free to wear what they wanted. Others preferred to see their nurses' faces. Not one person mentioned the extreme risk of infection posed by such garments.

As the discussion went on, my mind swam back to an incident at a European conference, where I'd met some cardiothoracic surgeons from the Middle East.

There were five of them: four men and a woman. The woman was clad in a black 'burka,' but not with the niquab, so her face was visible.

As a past president of the *European Association for Cardio-Thoracic Surgery,* it was appropriate that I welcome them – especially as nobody else was talking to them, and they looked lonely.

So, I ambled over, introduced myself, and greeted them, one by one, by shaking their hands.

The last one was the lady doctor – who smiled but, when I moved to shake hands, pulled sharply away.

"I am sorry, Professor," she said. "I cannot shake hands with you, for I do not shake hands with men."

"Forgive me, Doctor," I said. "I hope I didn't offend you."

"No, no – not at all. It is because of my religion."

"Of course."

A bell rang, and we went off to our different lectures.

The next day was the last day of the conference. After the coffee break, I decided to sit in the wide, pleasant atrium, in front of a large exhibition area.

The exhibitors were packing up, closing their displays, putting devices in boxes, and preparing to leave.

As I sat, writing a report on the conference, there was a swirl of darkness, like giant shadow, coming towards me.

It was the lady doctor I'd met the previous day.

"May I sit and have a word, please?"

"By all means."

"I do not shake hands with men," she began, "other than my husband, my brothers and my father. This is not only because of Islam, it is also my own decision."

"That's quite all right." I said. "No problem at all. You must do as you see fit."

Then a story my granddad told me popped into my mind. It was about a friend of his, named Moussa, who was Jewish and lived in the suburbs of Tehran.

In 1937, propaganda from Hitler's Germany had reached Iran, claiming that, like Germans, Iranians belonged to the Aryan race. Muslim Iranians were 'true Iranians,' but Jewish Iranians were not, because they were Semites.

Moussa was a merchant who lived modestly with his wife and two children. The children, like other non-Muslim kids, were often abused at school.

According to Moussa, only one of his children's teachers was tolerant. This man, although religious and high in the

Islamic hierarchy, was nice to Moussa's Jewish children, and helped them to achieve good grades.

He also advised Moussa to keep them at home during Islamic religious holidays. He had to make sure they didn't travel to the holy cities on rainy days because droplets of rainwater could spatter from their Jewish bodies on to the bodies of Muslims, contaminating them, and preventing them from entering the kingdom of heaven.

As I remembered my granddad's story, I noticed that the lady doctor was looking uncomfortable. I wondered if she was still troubled about the previous day's encounter.

"What is your name, Doctor?" I asked, breaking the silence.

"I am Sakineh."

I was surprised she gave me her first name instead of her family name. Then I remembered that, in some Middle Eastern cultures, it was a sign of respect for a young person to give his or her first name to an 'elder.'

In response, the elder would add the suffix 'Khanum' for a female, and 'Khan' for a male.

"Sakineh Khanum," I said. "I want you to know that I

am really not offended that you could not shake my hand yesterday."

"Thank you for your understanding," she said, lowering her eyes. "But I have come to see you for something else."

I waited to hear what it was.

She looked up. "I was wondering if you could help me in my career?"

Given the conversation we'd had the day before, my guess was she was going to specialise in gynaecology, and wanted an introduction to my brother – who was an eminent gynaecologist in the States.

"What are you going to specialise in?"

"I would like to be a urological surgeon, and wondered if you could help me find a job, for a year or so, in the UK."

To say this was unexpected would be an understatement. I had to weigh my words carefully.

"I see, well, this may be a little difficult..."

"I am a hard worker, and my husband is quite happy for me to do so," she declared.

"Do you know what urological surgeons do?"

"Yes, of course! And that is what I want to do."

"Dr Sakineh Khanum, because of your faith, you cannot shake hands with a strange man. What if you have to drain urine from a man's bladder? You will have to hold his penis."

She stared at me, shocked. “But I would never do that! I would do everything for females!”

I told her the bad news, as gently as I could.

“I’m afraid, Doctor, that here, in the United Kingdom, all urological surgeons treat both genders.”

26

MANSLAUGHTER

I first learned about it on the evening of the 29th of December 2005, when I was relaxing at home, sipping a glass of wine, and thinking back over the events of the year.

Although I was still working, I'd retired from the National Health Service, so wasn't expecting any emergency calls. The ringing phone was probably from a call-centre in India, which had purchased my details from Google, or Amazon, or some other website, and were now eager to tell me how I could make money as a day trader.

So, didn't answer it.

But the phone rang and rang until I thought it must be my elderly mother, calling from Geneva.

I set my wineglass down, and picked up the receiver.

"May I speak with Mr. Moghissi?" said a man's voice.

"How can I help you?"

"I'm a solicitor, and I've been asked to contact you by the MDU."[48]

[48] Medical Defence Union.

Really? Why?"

"A possible manslaughter case. I need some advice."

"What, now? It's ten o'clock at night. And it's practically New Year's Eve."

"Yes, I know. I'm awfully sorry but, you see, my client's being questioned tomorrow."

The client was a consultant surgeon suspected of killing a patient.

The solicitor told me the story.

In the early hours of the 10th of December, a man named Harold Palmer, who had a history of depression, tried to take his life by stabbing himself in the heart. His wife found him, called an ambulance, and he was rushed to hospital.

The paramedics left the knife in his chest during the patient's transport.

At the hospital, the A & E staff carried out first aid, until a senior consultant surgeon arrived and took charge. He examined the patient, looked at his X-rays, and decided the knife should be removed.

After a short discussion with his registrar, he withdrew the knife and, three minutes later, the patient died. Efforts were made to resuscitate him using CPR,[49] but to no avail.

[49] Cardio-Pulmonary-Resuscitation

The time of death was recorded as 9.20 a.m. on the 10th December, 2005. As expected, there was a post-mortem examination. What was *not* expected was the case being referred to the police.

The police asked everyone who'd witnessed the events to provide written statements, and then asked the consultant to come in for questioning.

The hospital authorities didn't offer the surgeon any legal assistance, so he turned to the Medical Defence Union for help. It was this organisation that had hired the solicitor I was now speaking to.

In preparing his client for the police interview, the solicitor had a list of questions he thought they might ask, and wanted my advice on how to answer them.

After hearing these hypothetical questions, I recommended his client stick to his written statement. The whole thing sounded bizarre to me and it was problematic, to say the least, for a senior consultant surgeon to be examined by police with no medical training.

The next day, the surgeon went to the police station with his solicitor. The line of questioning turned out to be just as the solicitor had foreseen. Accordingly, he took my advice and instructed his client – a Mr. Thornfield – to stick to his statement and make no further comments.

The interview lasted 15 minutes.

I was then hired as a medical expert, and received a transcript of the police interview, and the witness statements.

Early in the New Year, I received 700-plus pages of documents related to the case, and over 100 photos of the deceased, organ-by-organ, including photos of the heart taken from every angle.

A statement by the deceased's wife stated that, at about 7 am on the 10th of December 2005, she heard groaning and breathing so loud it woke her up. She rushed to her husband's bedroom, where she found him flat on the bed – blood everywhere – holding a knife deeply embedded in his chest.

She called 999.

The first constable to arrive described the scene as follows:

"Mr Gary Palmer was in his bedroom, lying diagonally across the bed. The brown handle of a knife, approximately 4 inches in length, was sticking out of the left side of the chest. It was in the area of the heart and was moving rhythmically, like the heart beat."

The victim was conscious, but restless and groaning, and trying to pull the knife from his chest. He had to be restrained, and his hands removed from the handle of the knife.

When the paramedics arrived, they carried out emergency procedures, put in an intravenous drip, and made sure not to disturb the knife. Then they took Mr. Palmer, by ambulance, to the District General Hospital.

The time of arrival at A&E was recorded as 8.15 a.m.

After studying the documents, it seemed to me that this was simply a successful suicide. What struck me as strange, though, was clear evidence that many of the witnesses were in collusion. The phraseology used on different witness statements was almost identical. And every witness – either openly or covertly – had accused the surgeon of killing the patient.

The first thing to do was confirm the knife really was in Gary Palmer's heart. So, I went to the photographs and the autopsy report.

I read the report several times and, each time, it seemed incomplete. The heart injuries, for example, were lacking in anatomical detail. Also, I wasn't persuaded that the pathologist had built a convincing picture of the cause of death. It looked as though he'd decided the haemorrhage was fatal before he did the autopsy.

Therefore, there was a case to be made for a second post-mortem – which I requested.

The second autopsy was done by an independent pathologist, who I asked to look into certain areas in the heart, which the first pathologist had omitted to examine.

The report of this autopsy was sent to me, and it answered my queries. More detailed than the first, it revealed that the death of Gary Palmer was not due to the surgeon's withdrawal of the knife.

There were 3 stab wounds in the anterior aspect of the chest wall. The first had penetrated the skin only. The second had pierced the left lung. The third had gone through the chest wall and entered the pericardium.[50]

There was a single, small incision in the pericardium, which had produced no more than 50 millilitres of blood inside this 'sack' that encloses the heart.

Although Mr. Palmer stabbed himself three times, there were *five* wounds: 1) the skin puncture, 2) the lung puncture, 3) a superficial wound penetrating less than a centimetre into the heart muscle, 4) a deeper cut into the muscular part of the wall between the two ventricles[51], and 5) a perforation of the left ventricle and a severing of the sub-valvular muscular structure in the interior of the heart, disrupting the anatomical integrity of the mitral valve[52] between the two chambers of the heart.

[50] The membrane that covers the heart like a sack.

[51] Inter-ventricular septum.

[52] The Mitral valve separates the upper left heart chamber from the lower left heart chamber, and helps control blood flow through the heart.

In addition, there was evidence of a previous heart attack and substantial coronary disease.

In September, 2006, as I prepared my report, the police conducted a second interview with Mr. Thornfield – this time, by two Detective Constables.

When I read the transcript of the interview, I found it most peculiar. Here are a few examples:

"The purpose of the interview was to provide Dr Thornfield with an opportunity to give a full account of the event under investigation and to have the evidence put to him."

"Dr Thornfield will be presented with a future opportunity to make comments on any and all those statements presented to him and to clear up any ambiguities that he believes may exist."

"A full file was submitted to the Crown Prosecution Service who have reviewed it in relation to statements obtained. CPS advised they would like the defendant to be given the opportunity to hear what other people have said because he had not access to this information. CPS was not prepared to make a final decision on whether or not Dr Thornfield should be charged at this time."

Charged with what? I was baffled.

To me, the narrative was as follows: Mr. Gary Palmer doesn't want to live anymore, so he tries to kill himself. His wife, several policemen, paramedics, and hospital staff try to save him – but fail. Were mistakes made? Possibly. But anyone reading the depositions could have no doubt that everyone – including Mr. Thornfield – did their best to save his life.

By the end of March 2007, I'd finished my report. Based on the findings of the second post-mortem, my hypothesis was that, at the time of withdrawal, the knife was not in the heart but in the pericardial sac.

I argued that if, at the time of its withdrawal, the knife was in the heart, there should have been a large volume of blood in the pericardial cavity – which was not the case.

Although there were two litres of blood in the left chest, this could not have come from bleeding caused by removal of the knife because only three minutes elapsed between withdrawal of the knife and the patient's death.

If this blood had come from the heart it would have had to pass through the hole in the pericardium caused by the knife. But this hole was too small for two litres of blood to have passed through it in 3 minutes.

There was also a discrepancy. Three wounds in the heart, but only *one* in the pericardium.

For me, this meant that one stab had pierced the chest wall, punctured the pericardium and entered the heart. The movement of the heartbeat had then pushed the knife out into the pericardium. Next, the knife, as it rose and fell with the breath, caused two further injuries.

So, to repeat: I was postulating that Mr. Palmer had stabbed himself three times, but only at the third attempt was the knife pushed into the heart. The knife then left the heart but remained in the pericardium, injuring the heart twice more.

In order to prove my theory, I had to address three issues:

1) What was the cause of death if not by acute haemorrhage?

2) How could my hypothesis explain the presence of two litres of blood in the chest, when no blood was found in the pericardium?

3) Where was the source of the haemorrhage if not the heart?

I constructed a rationale for my report, documented my arguments with published papers, and dispatched the report to the instructing solicitor.

The Crown Prosecution Service had decided to try the case in a Coroner's Court before determining whether or not to press criminal charges. The venue was a courtroom in the town of Chester-Le-Street, North Yorkshire.

The trial was set for October 8-11.

The only thing I knew about Chester-Le-Street was it had a viaduct. So, a few days before I was due to embark, I used Google to get some information on the place.

The main thing to remember was to pronounce 'le' as 'lee'. Chester-*Lee*-Street. This didn't surprise me because, in

1954, when I first came to England, I stayed in a village in the New Forest, near a town called Beaulieu, which everyone called 'Bewley.' I was saying it the French way until a garage-owner told me that, in England, French names are never pronounced the way they are in France.

On the afternoon of October 10th, armed with a suitcase of documents, and two sheets of Google's information on Chester-Le-Street, I set off to the battlefield.

Accommodation had been booked at the Lumley Castle Hotel, where I was also scheduled to have dinner with the instructing solicitor.

When I stepped down from the train at Chester-Le-Street, I entered a deafening nightmare of gale force winds and bucketing rain. There was no-one on the platforms, no-one in the dark station buildings. No-one anywhere.

I had a raincoat, hat, and an umbrella, but these couldn't cope with the ferocity of the downpour. Everything was getting soaked. And when I opened my umbrella, the wind snapped it inside out, and broke several spokes.

I left the umbrella on the platform, sad to see it go. It had given sterling service. But a broken umbrella in the pouring rain is like a lame horse in the Wild West. You have to shoot it and leave it for the buzzards.

I pulled down my hat and headed out of the station.

According to British Rail, there was a taxi stand outside the station entrance. I struggled through the storm trying to find it. Finally, I spotted a tiny taxi-stand sign. But there were no taxis.

Then I saw a notice: *Please pick up the phone and you will be connected to the Taxi Office.*

So that's what I did.

It was ringing. Good. And it kept on ringing. As it rang and rang, I got wetter and wetter. Standing alone in the wind and rain, with a dripping phone to my ear, I had an eerie sensation that I'd passed into a parallel world where I was the only human alive, and was ringing nowhere *from* nowhere.

I left the deserted station and walked down a steep road flooded with water. The wheel of my wheely suitcase submerged as I dragged it behind me.

Then I saw someone. A young woman with a pram, dashing along the pavement.

I hurried towards her.

"Excuse me! I'm terribly sorry to stop you in this weather, but..." I explained my plight.

"Oh dear," she said. "You need to get to the roundabout. It's left at the bottom, and then straight. The taxi rank is on one of the exit roads."

I thanked her, and dragged my suitcase 400 yards to the

bottom of the road, where I came to a drenched, demoralised roundabout. On one side of it was a public house with chairs and tables outside – blown over by the wind. On the other side, was a taxi stand with no taxis.

I went into the pub to get out of the rain. The place was empty. There were no customers. Just a single, mournful man lurking behind the bar.

"Do you know where I could get a taxi?" I asked him.

"No taxis in this weather."

"Could I phone for one"?

"Ain't got a number. Try the taxi office. Next to the Chinese take-away. Other side of the roundabout."

I sighed, went out and, leaning into the wind, sloshed through the rain to the other side of the roundabout. No buses, no cars, no human beings, no dogs, no cats – only empty streets with gushing streams competing to get to the nearest drain.

And no sign of the rain letting up.

Next to a closed Chinese take-away, was a door with 'TAXI' on it. I knocked for what seemed like an age, and was about to give up when a man's head appeared from a window.

"Do you know where I can get a taxi?" I shouted up to him.

"Wait there. I'm coming down!"

A few minutes later, the man came out, and led me to a parked car. He opened the door.

"Thank you," I said, climbing in.

The journey took 25 minutes and, as I was dropped off in front of what looked like Dracula's castle, there was a lightning flash, followed by a clap of thunder.

I entered the hotel – a luxurious conversion of a genuine 14th century castle – and, as I approached the reception desk, the well-groomed female receptionist saw me and frowned. No doubt I looked like the proverbial drowned rat.

After registering, I was shown to my room on the first floor. The décor was red and green, the chairs and settee velvety, and the bed was a four-poster.

My dinner engagement with Mr. Charles Lamb, the solicitor, was for 8 pm. It was now 8.20. It had taken me as long to get from the station to the hotel, as to get from Hull to Chester-Le-Street! I wanted to freshen up, but there was no time. I was late.

I hurried down the stairs to the dining room.

The restaurant was surprisingly crowded. Where had all these people come from? Mr. Lamb saw me – guessed I was the expert witness – and gave me a wave. I went over to his table. We'd spoken on the phone, but this was the first time we'd met.

We greeted each other, shook hands, sat down, and prepared to order. Charles Lamb was a youthful, well-mannered man in his mid-forties. I took to him straightaway.

As we ate, he updated me on the events in the court.

He described Day One, which had been wasted in positioning and posturing by the legal teams.

His account made me laugh. It reminded me of the fighting cocks I'd seen as a child on my grandfather's farm. The cockerels would wake just before sunrise, and crow at the tops of their voices. One cockerel always crowed first, followed by the second, and then the third. There was a hierarchy of crowing.

One day, I heard the third cock crow first. This was so unprecedented that I looked out the window and saw the three cocks in the farmyard, up on their toes, outraged, circling one another, wings half extended, fluffing, puffing, and pushing out their chests.

Mr. Lamb was not pleased by how things were going. What troubled him most was his client, Mr. Thornfield, who never stopped complaining. He described his manner as 'obnoxious.'

At about 11 pm, we decided to turn in, and arranged to meet for breakfast. We would go into court together. The plan was to have a short pre-court conference with the barrister and Mr. Thornfield – to whom I'd be introduced.

That night, I found it hard to sleep, so I looked at the records and my report. Eventually, I dropped off with the report in my hand.

I must have turned off the bedside light because, later, I awoke in darkness with a sense that someone was in the room. I don't know if I was awake or dreaming, but what I saw was a woman dressed like someone from the 14th century. She was exploring the corners of the room, looking for something.

I felt I should have reacted to this, but I was so tired I didn't bother!

At 6 am, I got up and, after the usual ablutions, made my way to the dining room, to have breakfast. After breakfast, when I was back in my room, I prepared for battle by playing in my head the opening bars of Beethoven 5th Piano Concerto (The Emperor) with hand gestures, as though I were conducting. I find this as an effective way to summon up courage, and am happy to recommend it.

Charles Lamb drove us to the court, where Mr. Thornfield, his wife, his legal team, and I, had a conference in the corridor.

This left me uneasy about Mr. Thornfield, who was both argumentative and overbearing. The barrister and I glanced at each other, but didn't say anything.

At 9.30 a.m., we entered the courtroom.

The Defence sat on one side of the benches; the lawyers for the Crown Prosecution, and their medical experts, sat on the other.

Behind us were members of the hospital staff, and their legal teams, the ambulance staff, and their legal team, the police, and their representatives, the family of the deceased, with their barristers, various journalists, and members of the public.

The clerk announced the arrival of the Coroner, who looked openly grumpy. This may have been due to the mountain of dossiers piled on his desk. I daresay my, rather lengthy, report was one of them.

The first person to be called was the A&E anaesthetist in charge of the patient before the arrival of Mr. Thornfield. He was asked to describe the sequence of events on the morning of the 10th of December.

He said they were careful not to move the knife and fought hard to improve the patient's condition.

"Soon after Mr. Thornfield's arrival, after a cursory examination of the patient, he looked at the X-rays," the anaesthetist said. "Then, after almost no discussion, he pulled the knife from the man's chest. Three minutes later, the patient died."

Next up was the Crown Prosecution's expert anaesthetist, who expressed his approval of the steps taken by the A&E staff.

He was asked to comment on the cause of death.

"I have no doubt it was due to a sudden haemorrhage caused by the withdrawal of the knife from the heart," he said.

"Are you saying the knife which had caused the injury was in fact plugging the hole in the heart caused by it, and its removal unplugged the hole resulting in acute haemorrhage?" asked the Coroner.

"Yes sir," he replied.

Next to appear was another expert witness for the CPS, Mr. Evelyn Villiers, a highly qualified cardiothoracic surgeon.

Mr. Villiers declared he was critical of the ambulance crew for taking the patient to the District General Hospital, instead of the nearby Cardiothoracic Surgical Centre.

After this, he addressed the A&E's management of the patient, which he said was exemplary.

Finally, he criticised Mr. Thornfield for withdrawing the knife, and stated he had little doubt that it was this that had caused the fatal haemorrhage.

He was asked if he could explain the small volume of blood in the pericardium, to which the answer was that the blood had simply poured out into the left chest.

Then, he referred to the withdrawal of the knife.

"In such cases, the knife should only be withdrawn when the chest is surgically opened and all necessary equipment is ready and on standby."

The questioning went on:

Doctor, are you familiar with the working of the ambulance and paramedic services"?

Can you comment on the consequence of the injuries to the valve of the heart in this case?"

What about the coronary arterial disease which, according to the pathologist, was considerable?"

Some of Mr. Villiers' answers were excellent. Others, I felt, were vague.

Then it was my turn to enter the witness box.

The Coroner asked if I was conversant with the background of the case and had access to all the relevant documents.

I responded in the affirmative.

"Your colleague, Mr. Evelyn Villiers, was critical of the ambulance crew and some of the paramedics for taking Mr. Palmer, to the District General Hospital instead of to the nearby Cardiothoracic Centre. Have you any comments to make on that?"

"Yes sir. Basically, the ambulance crew and paramedics

follow the rules. They don't make the rules. They were told to take the casualty to DGH and they did so. Their job is to exercise their professional duty to give first aid, and transport the patient to a designated hospital. The records show that they discharged this duty effectively. Can you, sir, imagine a scenario in which the ambulance crew and paramedics had used their initiative and taken the patient to the cardiothoracic surgery centre, and the patient had died enroute? They would now be standing accused."

According to Charles Lamb, this was the first time the Coroner stopped looking grumpy.

The Coroner thanked me, and turned to the barrister for the paramedics, asking him if he wanted to question me before we moved on.

"No sir, the professor has answered the question to our satisfaction," he replied.

The Coroner then peered at me and said: "You've had the opportunity to read the witness statements of those present in the A&E Department on the morning of the 10th of December 2005. You have also examined the X-rays and the report of the pathologist, as well as the autopsy photographs. Can you tell the court whether you believe, like Mr. Villiers, that the initial management of the patient at A&E, before the arrival of Mr. Thornfield was exemplary?"

"No sir, I can't. Would you allow me to expand on this?"

"Go ahead."

"The A&E staff acted according to the guidelines for serious injury cases: ABC – Airway, Breathing and Circulation. However, I do not go as far as Mr. Villiers in describing their actions as exemplary because, although the staff acted according to the principles of ABC, in the case of chest injuries there is a 4th acronym, the letter D – standing for Drainage of the chest. The X-rays of the patient indicated hydro-pneumothorax[53], which should have been drained by inserting a tube in the chest. This was not done."

The Coroner then asked what I thought about the actions of Mr. Thornfield. "Do you think he should not have removed the knife from the heart?"

"As a general rule, a sharp instrument suspected to be in the heart, should only be withdrawn when the patient is on the operating table, with a competent surgeon at the helm. But, in this case, my opinion is that Mr. Thornhill was justified in using his own judgement in withdrawing the knife because it was not in the heart. It was in the pericardium. Therefore, its removal could not cause a fatal haemorrhage."

There was silence. Looks were exchanged. And the

[53] Fluid and air outside the lung in the chest.

journalists began scribbling.

The Coroner asked if I'd read the autopsy letter in which the Home Office pathologist had proposed a 99% probability that death was caused by a haemorrhage resulting from the knife being removed from the heart. Could I comment on this?

Yes, I could.

"With the greatest respect, I must state that there are a number of paradoxes. In his report, the pathologist states there is a reasonable possibility that Mr Palmer's death, after the withdrawal of the knife, was a coincidence. Later, when pressed, he wrote that 'it was not within his remit to give an opinion on the likelihood of the two incidents occurring coincidentally.' Again, he was pressed and, this time, he said that, on balance, there was a 99% probability that death occurring soon after withdrawal of the knife was *not* coincidental but consequential. In my view, the pathologist may not have appreciated the hemodynamic alterations resulting from injuries to the mitral valve. I therefore respectfully submit that hemodynamics – which forms the scientific basis of fluid motion – has not been taken into account."

"Very well," said the Coroner. "Would you explain the cause of death, and the part that the withdrawal of the knife played in it?"

"Yes, sir. I believe death was caused by heart failure due to mitral valve incompetence, affecting adversely the cardiac output, which was further reduced by extensive coronary arterial disease, and haemorrhage through the injury. The blood in the chest had been collecting long before the withdrawal of the knife. The removal of the knife by Mr. Thornfield was not significant. The two litres of blood in the chest could not have been delivered from the pericardium in only three minutes through a 2-centimetre opening."

Next, the Coroner asked if the barrister from the CPS, and the barrister representing the family, wanted to question me. They both answered 'yes'.

The barrister for the family asked: "Do you think if Mr. Palmer had been taken straight to a cardiothoracic unit instead of the District General Hospital, he would have survived?"

"Regrettably, no. Repair of the heart would not, in my view, have been compatible with survival because of the disrupted mitral valve, and substantial Coronary arterial disease."

"Could the cardiac surgeon not have dealt with those as well?" he asked.

"Technically yes, but I don't think Mr. Palmer would have survived such a major procedure."

Then it was the turn of the barrister for the CPS to question me. He began by asking about my experience with stab wounds of the heart.

"Have you dealt with many such cases before?" he asked.

"I've had about 50 serious cases, of which roughly half survived. The survivors were aged below 50 and usually had no intra-cardiac structural damage, or serious pre-existing coronary vascular disease."

"Professor, what is the basis on which you suggest that the blood in the chest was *not* the result of withdrawal of the knife and sudden haemorrhage?"

"It's based on two pieces of evidence. Firstly, that the bleeding from the heart had to pass through the pericardium, which had a small 2cm hole in it created by the knife. Cardiac arrest occurred three minutes after removal of the knife, so the two litres of blood had to have filled the left chest in three minutes. The calculation of the flow rate through the 2cm hole, using a hydrodynamic physics equation, shows that only 150-200 millilitres of blood could have exited the pericardium, not 2 litres. Secondly, the pericardium contained only about 50 grams of blood. One would expect much more than that if there'd been a sudden acute haemorrhage in the heart."

He went on to ask me about my evidence that the knife was in the pericardium and not the heart.

"There are two reasons that suggest the knife was in the pericardium when Mr. Thornfield withdrew it," I said. "First, the registrar noted that the knife handle was moving with the breathing – not with the heart rate. And, second, there is one 2cm incision in the pericardium but three wounds in the heart. The orientation of only one of these fits with the pericardial wound. The other two are smaller and of different orientations. How can one explain this other than by the knife being out of the heart but staying in the pericardium to wound the heart twice more?"

The barrister was quick to rise again. Almost as soon as my last word was pronounced, he said:

"The deceased could have stabbed himself three times in the heart through the same hole."

This was so unbelievable that I said: "You'd have to be Houdini to do that!"

The public gallery burst out laughing. I glanced at the Coroner, who was waiting for the laughter to die down.

Then he said: "If there are no further questions for the professor, we will adjourn for lunch."

I climbed down from the witness box, and was accosted by several journalists asking me how to spell my name.

The legal team expressed satisfaction with my witness box efforts, but Mr. Thornfield made no comment. In fact, he gave me the impression that he didn't agree with my hypothesis.

There was something old-fashioned about him. He was like a doctor who'd worked for years in the colonies. From the witness statements, I'd learned he was unpopular at his hospital. Many of his co-workers considered him a tyrant.

I glanced at his wife – clearly shattered by the whole thing – and couldn't help feeling sorry for her.

Charles Lamb, the solicitor, told me I didn't need to stay, and that he'd call me later with the final summation. Pleasant and courteous, he found me a taxi, and accompanied me to the station.

The storm had now blown itself out, and the station, which had seemed so dismal the night before, was sparkling in the sunshine. What a difference a day makes! (Although there were still no taxis at the taxi stand.)

The following afternoon, Charles Lamb phoned to tell me that Mr. Thornfield had been cleared of any blame in the death of Gary Palmer.

I put down the receiver and mused over the whole expensive, and protracted, episode.

Why had it happened?

Thornfield was a good surgeon. The fault didn't lie there. No, the fault lay in his high-handed attitude. If he'd only been nicer to his staff, he, and his wife, could have avoided the entire ordeal.

My first thought – that it was absurd to charge this doctor with manslaughter – had been right but, on reflection, it seemed there was a charge of manslaughter to be answered.

Not manslaughter of the sick, suicidal Gary Palmer, but the manslaughter of Mr. Thornfield.

The man Mr. Thornfield was slaughtering was himself.

27

FRED

When I first saw Fred, I thought I was seeing a cowboy out of a John Wayne film.

But he wasn't from the Wild West. He was a farmer who lived alone in the wilds of North Yorkshire, with large herds of cattle.

A week earlier, he'd coughed up blood, and his GP had referred him to my NHS clinic.

But Fred, not wanting to waste time – and very much against a Yorkshireman's principles – had chosen a private consultation.

When I sent my secretary to the waiting room to fetch him, she came back saying there was no-one there.

"No-one there?"

She shook her head.

"Let's give it a few more minutes, and, if he doesn't show up, we'll call it a day."

A few minutes later, I went to the waiting room myself.

When I opened the door, I saw a tall, rough-looking man dressed like a rancher, in a beaten-up, ankle-length raincoat.

"How can I help you?" I said

"I 'arr a perment," he said.

"Excuse me?"

The way he spoke was almost incomprehensible. It was even hard for my secretary to understand – and she was born and bred in Yorkshire.

After an unintelligible interview, I asked to examine him. He shed his raincoat and his moleskin jacket, revealing a ring of bulging sacks hanging from his belt. Seeing my perplexity, he told me he'd just come from the cattle market, and the sacks were stuffed with bank notes.

After my examination, I suspected the worst, and urged him to have some tests.

These were done and when the reports came in, they verified my fears. He had lung cancer.

I scheduled him as quickly as possible, and carried out an operation which removed the tumour, together with the section of lung that contained it. Everything went well and, being a strong, vigorous man, it wasn't long before he recovered.

As with all my cancer patients, I continued to see him in a series of follow-ups.

About a year later, the phone rang and it was Fred, the North Yorkshire cowboy. As usual, I could barely understand him, but it was obvious something was wrong.

I asked him to drop by the hospital.

"Nay, ai see ye a da fiss nigh tha pub."

Having known him for a while, I was able to decipher this as him wanting to see me at my private consulting rooms, which were opposite a pub.

I saw him there that afternoon, and found him in great pain, thanks to several fractured ribs. He'd been kicked by one of his 'old girls' (a cow.)

"Okay, let's have a look at your chest."

I got his shirt off – not without some difficulty – and saw that his chest was strapped tightly in yards of animal bandage, holding three pieces of wood acting as splints. Fred had immobilised his chest to reduce the pain caused each time he took a breath. He was nothing if not ingenious.

I treated his pain with local anaesthetics, and then dealt with the fractures and soft tissue bruising.

Over the next six weeks, I drove out to his enchanting cottage in the wilderness, to administer local anaesthetics in the areas of his rib fractures, and to monitor his progress.

The simplicity of Fred's life and his love of nature, fascinated me. He lived in a different world.

Oddly enough, he seemed to be as interested in me as I was in him, and asked me to visit whenever I liked. I took him up on this and, over the next two years, we became good friends.

Fred didn't have any children and, one day, he suggested he leave his cottage to me in his will. This was quite a surprise – and I was very touched – but I told him I couldn't possibly accept.

I don't know if he ever made a will but, if he did, I doubt it was recorded with a solicitor.

Knowing Fred, he would have written it on a scrap of paper, put it in an old tin, and placed it on a rafter in the cowshed.

28

THE ALPINE HAT

Throughout the '70s and '80s, I went into my hospital on Saturdays for a walk around the wards. I did this to check up on patients who'd just had their operations, and to boost the morale of the nurses who, on weekends, tended to feel neglected by the senior staff.

For these visits, I would dress more casually than during the week. But I still wore my bow tie. My bow tie wasn't the type with stiff wings going out horizontally, which I think looks like a toy aeroplane's propeller. It was a floppy one, with 'butterfly wings' drooping down.

With this softer type of bow-tie, which you tie yourself, you can create different 'looks' depending on how you tie it. On work days, I'd tie the knot in a solemn way. On weekends, or when going out for lunch, I'd make it floppier – conveying a more relaxed approach.

You can't do this with a ready-made bow tie. Not that I ever wore a ready-made. A senior consultant once told me: "If you can't tie a bow tie, you shouldn't be wearing one!"

When I drove to the hospital on Saturdays, I parked my

car in the reserved parking space, got out, and then – rain or shine – would go for a stroll down a gravel path that led to the boundary of the hospital's estate. I liked this path because it led through a cheerful, bucolic area, dominated by mature trees. It was like being out in the country.

At the end of the path was a building housing the X-ray department. Beyond this, and to the left, stood the gardener's hut, which bordered an apple orchard, and a field where Mr. Boyce, the gardener, grew vegetables for the patients and staff.

Sometimes I found Mr. Boyce in his little hut, and I'd stop off for a chat. He'd made the hut very comfortable. It was especially pleasant in winter when, thanks to a wood-burning stove, it was warm and toasty.

For these short promenades, I put on a hat, and took one of the walking sticks I kept in my car. I was always accumulating walking sticks. Also hats. I had a collection of hats – about two dozen – which came from different countries where I'd given lectures.

Usually, these hats were given to me as presents although, now and again, I'd give into temptation and buy one myself. My favourite, for my Saturday morning walks, was an Alpine hat with a sprightly feather in it.

After my stroll, I'd go to the office, leave the hat and the walking stick there, and head towards the wards.

For several years, I had a patient, named Ernie, who suffered from bilateral pulmonary emphysema, and frequent lung collapses.

Emphysema is a chronic disease in which the lungs lose their elasticity resulting in the air chambers (alveoli) becoming over-inflated with air, and their walls becoming thin.

The thinned walls, and swollen air sacks, become like little balloons, forming air cysts. Ruptures in the walls of these cysts allow air to escape into the chest (pleural cavity), causing the lung to collapse – which can be life-threatening.

Ernie's lungs were badly damaged, and one or other of his lungs would collapse as often as six times a year. Unhappily, his condition couldn't be treated with reparative surgery. All we could do was siphon the air out of his chest cavity, so the lung could re-inflate.

We made an arrangement so Ernie could by-pass A&E, and come straight into the ward, whenever he recognised the signs of an imminent attack.

Ernie was a lively, warm-hearted man who people loved to joke with. He was never a bother to the nursing staff, and would often help them, when he was able – even if there was a drainage tube in his chest!

On one of my Saturday rambles, I popped into the X-ray department to look at his most recent X-rays, which had been taken that morning.

They looked good.

Later, in the ward, one of the first people I bumped into was Ernie.

"Well, hello Ernie, how are things?" I said.

"I'm OK, guv."

"I've just seen your X-rays. They're fine. You can go home as soon as you like. Take your medication, and see me in the clinic in 3 weeks' time. And, of course, the door's always open if you need to come in."

Ernie thanked me, and shook my hand.

Then he said: "I saw you out there, walking. I like your hat. Very nice. Very smart. I'd love a hat like that. If I knew where I could get one, I'd ask my family to chip in, and buy one for Christmas."

After I finished my ward rounds, I asked the sister if she'd bring Ernie to my office as soon as he was packed and ready for discharge.

A little later, he appeared, and I picked up my Alpine hat and gave it to him to try on. He did so, and it fitted him perfectly.

I took him to the little side room of my office, so he could see himself in the mirror.

"Don't I look important!" he said.

I said it suited him better than me, so the hat was his.

When he looked at me, his expression almost made me weep.

Several years later, I had a letter from Ernie's daughter saying her father had passed away.

She told me he'd left a note asking her not to dispose of the hat, but to keep it in the family.

That's when I wept.

29

MY FIRST PATIENT

In 1954, I came to Britain, from Switzerland, as a post-graduate medical student. My first job was as a House Surgeon at Edgware General Hospital in North West London.

After my appointment, I resolved to go to the hospital two days early to become familiar with the job, and the routines of the wards.

On Sunday – before the Monday I was due to start work – I entered the Sister's Office in the male ward, and came across an attractive nurse in her mid 30's.

I introduced myself.

"Why are you here today?" she asked, surprised.

"Well, I thought I'd come in and look at the patients' records. See what kind of cases I'm going to be dealing with."

She looked at me. She seemed to be considering something.

"Dr M," she said, "can you do intra-arterial injections?"

"Intra-arterial?" I said, guardedly. "Which artery?"

She explained that my consultant was interested in vascular problems – especially those of the leg and foot – and had devised a saline solution, which he injected daily, for a week, into the femoral artery of his patients with vascular deficiencies.

She told me one of my tasks – once I'd done 4 weeks' training – would be to administer this intra-arterial treatment.

"I look forward to learning it," I said. "I've done blood transfusions at the Geneva Transfusion Centre, so I should be able to learn it in a couple of weeks."

She told me that, as the previous house surgeon had gone, she was going to call the Registrar to give the injections.

"Fine," I said. "I'll stay around and watch."

She picked up the phone and asked for the registrar.

The operator told her Mr. Lewis was busy in theatre.

This was a problem.

She glanced at me, made a decision, and asked me to follow her. Curious, I went with her, down the corridor to the treatment area. Here I saw – laid out on a tray – a host of syringes and vials of the drug, covered by a sterile towel.

"I'm not allowed to do the injection," she said, "because I'm not a doctor."

"Oh?"

"Could *you* do it?"

"Me?"

"I'll show you how."

"You know how to do it?"

"Of course! I've seen it done a hundred times!"

This was tricky. I could be getting myself into hot water. This was my first professional job – and I hadn't even started yet. Was I going to screw everything up before I'd even started?

'Oh well,' I thought. 'I may as well get on with it!'

We walked to the ward, where we found a skinny young man seated in a chair. His left leg was resting on a stool, and his foot was loosely wrapped in cotton wool.

"This is Dr M, our new house surgeon," announced the sister, stripping off the cotton wool. "He can do your injection today."

The young man's foot was not pretty. The big toe and little toe had been amputated, leaving only three bruised-looking digits.

The Sister and I had agreed to inform the patient that I hadn't given this type of injection before, so I asked him:

"Are you willing to let me do it?"

"Don't feel you have to," the sister chimed in. "The registrar will be along later, and he can do it then."

"Hey, if you think it's all right," said the young man. "Go for it. The worst that can happen is I lose another toe!"

"Very well," said the sister. "I'm now going to show the doctor how it's done, but don't worry – even though he hasn't done it before, he's done lots of blood transfusions in Geneva."

"Fancy that!" grinned the young man. "All the way from Geneva just to give me my injection!"

So, a little nervously, I scrubbed, put on a pair of surgical gloves, and picked up the syringe.

Under the Sister's instructions, I palpated the patient's femoral artery and inserted the needle into it. Then, I tested the insertion by observing the jets of arterial blood with each pulse.

Next, I injected the mixture.

Finally, when the syringe was empty, I withdrew it and replaced it on the tray.

I was immensely relieved. I'd even managed to do it without hesitating or shaking.

Then we moved on to the second patient, and repeated the procedure.

Three patients later, with all the injections completed, the sister and I returned to the nurses' office – both elated. I could have hugged her, but controlled myself, and simply thanked her for her tuition.

"You know," she said, "I tried to teach the last house

surgeon but he wouldn't listen to me because I'm only a ward sister. He wanted to learn it from the registrar."

"And did he?" I asked.

"Oh yes. Eventually. But it took ages because our registrar's always so busy. And he'd generally do the injections himself because it was quicker that way."

The next morning, Monday – my first official day on the job – I met my consultant, and accompanied him on his rounds.

"I've heard what you did yesterday," he told me.

I froze.

Seeing my uneasiness, he chuckled. "No, no." He patted me on the back. "You did a good job. Well done!"

He told me the patient with the three toes had asked him if he could always be given his injection by 'the new doctor.'

And, later that afternoon, this same patient called for me and handed me a small box of chocolates, given to him by his family.

"This is to thank you for my injection," he said. "I didn't feel a thing."

I was so touched by this gesture that I wanted to share it with the sister. So, I went to her office, and presented her with the box of chocolates.

"What's this for?" she said.

"To thank you for having confidence in a novice."

30

THE SNEAKY SISTER-IN-LAW

Pete was a 41-year-old businessman, married with three young children. For some time, he'd had a pain in his chest and problems swallowing. But he hadn't seen a doctor because he was working hard to expand his business and support his family.

Eventually, when he couldn't swallow even soft food, he went to his General Practitioner. The GP set up appointments for X-rays and an endoscopy.

These tests revealed he had oesophageal cancer.

After seeing an oncologist who pronounced him unsuitable for chemotherapy or radiation, he was referred to me. Sadly, the cancer was so advanced that he wasn't suitable for surgery either. All we could do was employ methods to allow him to swallow, and receive nutrients, and treat him for pain.

For several months, we did the best we could, but nothing could save him, and he passed away.

I was distressed by Peter's death. It's always very upsetting when a man dies young, leaving small children fatherless.

Throughout his last days, he spoke at length about his wife, parents, and children. He was acutely aware of the trouble his death was going to cause them.

During his illness, I also got to know his wife, Janet, a strong woman who fought bravely to control her emotions so as not to alarm her kids. They were lucky to have her – a mother capable of being both a mother *and* a father. I could even see her running Pete's business.

A few weeks after the funeral, I received a letter from Peter's sister. It was hand-written and six pages long.

After telling me she worked as an agency nurse, she wrote: "I am finding strength at this very sad time of Peter's death," and then went on to describe a long list of ailments for which she was seeing a surgeon at Charing Cross Hospital, in London.

Five pages of the letter were all about herself!

She said she was sorry she wasn't able to visit Peter during the last 18 months of his life, when he'd been ill, and then asked me for copies of his medical records, my correspondence with his GP, and his post-mortem report.

Why did she want all that?

There was more: could I please telephone her, so we could have a chat? Could I get in touch with her surgeon in London? And would I swear not to breathe a word of this to her sister-in -law?

'Is that all, madam?' I thought.

I wrote back saying I was not at liberty to send her Peter's medical notes, or his post-mortem results, without:

a) obtaining authority from his wife, and

b) her surgeon writing to me requesting the data – and giving his reasons for wanting it.

I didn't like to worry Pete's wife, but I had to let her know about her sister-in-law's letter.

Soon afterwards, I received the following:

"I am sorry Pete's sister has troubled you with such a highly irregular request about the post-mortem. I most certainly do not wish to divulge any information regarding this to anyone, unless you yourself wished to do so."

I thought her very kind to say: '...unless you yourself wish to do so.' Of course, I had no wish to do so!

"I definitely would never give permission for information to be passed to any member of Pete's family. They were no support to either him or myself when he was so ill last year, and they have been no help to me in the last two months. And now they want to cause trouble at a time when I can least do with it.

Fortunately, I am blessed with the best friends, neighbours and family (on my side) I could wish for, who have all been such a great support to me, and I am beginning to feel quite a lot better now.

I do apologise that you have been troubled with this matter."

All my love,

Janet.

31

ODE TO DELIVERANCE

My final year as an undergraduate at the Medical School in Geneva was 1953 – the most crowded, most memorable, and most insane year of my life.

It began like any other of my six previous years but, as soon as the New Year's festivities were over, I was filled with dread. There was a mountain of work ahead, followed by four months of continuous examinations.

When I think about it now – even after all these years – I still feel panicky. I don't believe anyone, who is not a college student in his final year, can imagine what the pressure is like.

Adrenaline floods the bloodstream, tachycardia is a fact of life, and a good night's sleep is a luxury won only after an exam is completed.

And, to add to the agony, I was haunted by the sacrifice my parents had made to send me to university. They'd worked hard, and suffered many privations, to give me this chance.

I could not let them down.

1953 was also my final year at the Conservatoire.[54] I'd

[54] Ecole Sociale de Musique de Geneve.

been having violin lessons since the age of eight, and my teachers had convinced my parents I could be a concert violinist. In fact, at that time, I wasn't sure if I wanted to be a doctor or a classical musician.

So, two finals in one year. I was bound to spontaneously combust!

Luckily, I was allowed to postpone the music examinations for six months and, as it turned out, working towards my music diploma was a holiday from my medical studies.

A change is as good as a rest.

When our professor – Maître Fernand Closset – the director of the Conservatoire, gave me permission to take the exams in December instead of June, he jokingly said:

"I've not handed the diploma to a doctor before. It would be amusing to hear the officials at the diploma ceremony calling you Dr. Moghissi."

I liked that idea too, but it meant *I had to pass both finals.*

January 1953 began with a review of each subject on the syllabus. These included anatomy, physiology, pathology, pharmacology, dermatology, medical practice, and surgery involving every system of the body. In all, there were 30 examinations. And, for most subjects, there were written, viva, and practical examinations.

Nothing was left out.

My major subjects were Pathology, Surgery, Medicine, Gynaecology, Obstetrics, Pediatric Medicine and Accident & Emergency. However, the professors of the minor subjects marked their papers so fiercely that students had to work hard on these minor subjects too.

On top of everything else, I received a long-awaited letter saying I'd been selected as a 'Stagiaire' at the Maternity Hospital. This meant I was to work as a resident/apprentice for a month, during which I'd learn how to carry out both normal and forceps deliveries.

During the residency, the student had to stay at the Maternity Hospital, with only one afternoon and evening off a week. However, my luck was in and, by special permission from Professor de Watteville,[55] (a music lover), I was given *two* evenings off a week, to attend rehearsals of the Conservatoire's orchestra.

We were rehearsing for a concert to be given at a grand auditorium called the Victoria Hall. The date of the concert was a week before the end of my residency at the Maternity Hospital.

The concert programme was structured in two parts, with an interval. The first part comprised of two works: *La*

[55] Professor Hubert de Watteville was the gynaecologist who, in 1968, delivered Sophia Loren's baby.

Pie Voleuse (The Thieving Magpie) by Rossini, and *Concerto for Trombone and Orchestra* by Rimsky-Korsakov.

A gifted, 17-year-old member of the Conservatoire, named Jean, would play the trombone solo.

The second part of the concert was Beethoven's *Ninth Symphony* (the Choral Symphony), which climaxes with the famous 'Ode to Joy.' The singing was to be done by the *Workers Union Chorus,* and *The Chorus of Ville de Genève.*

The solo parts were given to senior music students, and one professional soprano.

On the day of the concert, I'd taken my violin, and my 'penguin suit,' to the hospital, so I could change, grab a taxi, and get to the Victoria Hall by 4 pm.

At about 2 pm, I went to my room, put the mute on my violin to dampen the sound, and began practicing an étude by Paganini called *Perpetuum Mobile.*

This étude can be played at different speeds. You can also alter the bowing, and play it in different styles. I was just getting into it, when someone knocked on the door. I stopped, opened the door, and was confronted by a pretty student midwife who asked if I could go to the Delivery Room.

I hesitated, looked at my watch, saw I had an hour and a half before I had to be at the concert hall, and agreed to follow her.

In the Delivery Room, I was able to 'scrub' – a term used in an operating theatre to wash and brush (literally) the hands. Then, I put on a theatre gown, and sterile gloves, and prepared to deliver the baby.

I'd done deliveries before, but they'd all been done under supervision. This was my first 'solo flight' – and I was excited.

Things didn't go smoothly, however. Despite the yells of the midwives and nurses to "Push! Push! Push!" the baby refused to come.

Finally, I sent a nurse to find a senior doctor.

One of my supervisors arrived, took control, and guided me in the use of forceps. It took time, but I managed it without too much trauma to the baby or the mother. In fact, the patient thanked me for my 'gentle technique.'

My first forceps delivery!

That done, I rushed to the shower room, washed, got changed, took a cab to the Victoria Hall, ran through the 'Artists Entrance,' and down to the stage, where I hastily took my place in the orchestra next to Marianne, the lead violinist.

The auditorium was packed.

Marianne stood up and gave the lead's tune for La/A, followed by Mi/E, Re/D and Sol/G, and checked the sound of the ensemble.

Next, our beloved conductor, the famous Fernand Closset, arrived to thunderous applause.

Standing proudly in front of the orchestra, he bowed to the audience, then turning to us, he smiled, lifted his baton, and off we went.

There was no problem with the first part of the programme. Our Rossini charmed the audience, and Jean received prolonged applause for his trombone solo.

Then, it was the interval, during which I looked quickly at the score of the *Ninth Symphony*, and did the job I'd been given of checking that the right scores were on the music stands.

The audience returned and, back in our seats, we watched the soloist come on stage, followed by our conductor.

There were no difficulties with the first three movements of Beethoven's 9th. And the fourth movement, which our musicologist had told us was a 'symphony within a symphony,' went well, up until the start of the Recitative and Chorus. That was when the trouble started.

The orchestra and the singers went out of synch.

In rehearsals, Maître Fernand Closset, had foreseen that a miss-match between orchestra and singers might occur, and had told us what we should do. Thanks to this, and his skilful conducting, we got out of trouble – but it was quite a struggle.

We finished the concert, and the audience, which was composed mostly of parents of the students, and Friends of the Conservatoire, were happy and satisfied.

But, the next day, the city's newspaper – 'La Tribune de Genève' – while praising the concert as a whole, remarked that the last movement of Beethoven's *Ninth Symphony* was such hard going for the players that instead of 'Ode to Joy,' a more apt title would have been: 'Ode to Deliverance!'

Concert over, I returned to the Maternity Hospital, intending to go to bed early. But a group of nurses and student midwives (some of whom had been at the concert) crashed into my room and insisted on having a party.

So, that's how I celebrated my first big concert, and my first forceps delivery!

32

DON'T CALL ME A HERO

George Waters was a fifty-year-old engineer who worked in a local aviation factory, where he was known for being amiable, skilful and meticulous.

He wasn't ambitious, had no enemies, and loved his family. Rather than go drinking with his mates, he preferred to go home, and see his children – and be bossed around by his wife – which he thoroughly enjoyed. And when he joined his kids in a game of football, he was just like one of them.

But even a blameless man like George can be stricken by illness. In his case, it was cancer. When the news got out, everyone who knew him said: "Oh no, not him!"

A diagnosis of cancer often triggers feelings of doom so deep that the world stops spinning. All you can think of is: 'My life is over.'

Of the various types of cancer, one of the biggest killers is cancer of the lung. But it doesn't have to be a death sentence. If diagnosed and treated early, it can be cured.

Fortunately, George had a tumour that could be treated surgically. The only thing that concerned me was the chance there might be microscopic tumours in his lymph nodes.

At that time, my hospital didn't have the facilities to do CT scans, however a battery of other tests showed no detectable dissemination of cancer outside the lung.

The routine was to admit patients for surgery two days before the operation. This was to prepare them with counselling, breathing exercises, and physiotherapy.

George was admitted in early December.

His son, Jack, who was about 13, was very attached to his father, and disturbed by his absence from home. He knew his dad was going to have a 'big operation,' and it worried him so much, he couldn't concentrate at school. His mother told me he never stopped talking about cancer, the operation, the hospital, and his father's surgeon. He was telling everyone I was 'the greatest surgeon around.' (Well, who else could operate on his precious dad other than the greatest surgeon?)

On the day of the operation, everything went well, and George was discharged a week before Christmas.

Soon after this, I was told that a reporter at the local radio station had made a programme about local schools. In the course of this programme, he'd interviewed various pupils and asked them who their heroes were.

One of the boys he interviewed was George's boy, Jack. When asked: 'Who is your hero?' the reporter was expecting to hear the name of a famous footballer, or a rock star, but Jack said: "My hero is Doctor Moghissi because he was the one who gave my daddy back to us."

The broadcast was heard by some of the hospital staff, who told me about it.

This put me in a strange mood, and I went to my office and locked the door. I needed time on my own because a deep memory had been triggered.

It was when my mother fell seriously ill. I was seven years old, and her illness caused me so much anxiety that I wouldn't leave her bedside. Each time our family doctor came to visit, I tried to guess my mother's condition by the expression on his face.

When, after one of the doctor's visits, I heard him tell my grandmother that the danger had passed, I was filled with joy.

Two days before Christmas, I received the following letter from Jack.

Dear Mr Moghissi

I thank you for the ~~sterling~~ work you have done on my father. He is looking much better now than he has done for quite a while. I think you are a very clever man, and I hope you do many more operations as neat as the one performed on my dad.

My Mum and I love Dad very much and it makes us very grateful. With Christmas coming up, it would not have seemed like

Christmas without Dad. Oh, by the way, some of my form mates have been asking about dad and when I told them about you, one girl said: 'I don't know him but I'll bet he's dead clever.' How is that for a compliment, eh?

Yours Faithfully

Jack Waters

PS I crossed out sterling because with the value of sterling now, it's an insult to you!

Two years went by, and George's cancer came back. It spread and, a year later, he passed away. It was his wife who gave me the bad news.

I never heard from his son, Jack, again. No doubt, I was now a 'fallen hero.'

I still think of Jack sometimes, especially when I go to watch one of my grandsons play football. He plays in a junior team at Regents Park in London where we join scores of children, and their fathers, walking to the pitch.

My grandson notices when my mind slips back into the past. I feel him tug my hand, and hear him asking: "Are you all right, Grandad?"

And that brings me back to the here and now.

Professor Keyvan Moghissi

BSc., M.D., F.R.C.S.(Ed.), F.R.C.S.(Eng.), F.E.T.C.S.

Keyvan Moghissi is one of the UK's leading Cardiothoracic Surgeons, with many books, papers, articles and presentations to his name.

He obtained first class degrees at the *University of Geneva,* before embarking on postgraduate studies in General and Chest surgery in Switzerland and the UK.

His training continued at *Southampton Chest Hospital* and, as a Senior Research Fellow at the Department of Physiology and Biochemistry at *Southampton University,* where he won two Wessex Research Prizes. He was then awarded a Fellowship of the *Royal College of Surgeons* of Edinburgh. Following this, he worked in rotation between *Hammersmith, Harefield* and the *Great Ormond Street* Children's hospital in London.

In 1970, he was appointed Consultant Cardiothoracic Surgeon in Hull, with a mission to establish an open-heart surgery at *Castle Hill Hospital.*

In the 1970s and 1980s, KM became one of the Founding Fathers of the *Thoracic Surgical Club* and the *European Association of Cardio-Thoracic Surgery* (EACTS), for which he served as its second President. He also played a major role in the foundation of the *European Respiratory Society* (ERS).

In 1985, KM undertook pioneering laser surgery of the

chest, and was the first cardiothoracic surgeon to use a laser to remove secondary breast cancer from the lung without loss of lung tissue.

In 1989, he was part of an international team pioneering the use of *Photodynamic Therapy* (PDT) for lung cancer in the UK and Europe.

KM was key to the creation of the *Yorkshire Laser Centre* – the project of a charitable trust, *The Moghissi Laser Trust* (Reg charity no: 326689). He was also responsible for the foundation of the *European Platform for Photodynamic Medicine* (EPPM) in 2006, and became its first President.

KM has been honoured with membership of *L'Academie de Chirurgie* (Paris), an honorary Visiting Professorship from *Guang Zhou University* (China), and honorary membership of a number of other international and European Associations. His honours include awards for contribution to science and cardiothoracic surgery from Russia, and an Award for Life Long Contribution to Cardiothoracic Surgery from the *World Society of Cardiothoracic Surgery.*

KM's hobbies include languages, classical music, and playing the violin.

He studied music in parallel with his school and medical studies and, in 1954, qualified in Violin under Professor Fernand Closset (Diplome de Capacité), at the *Conservatoire Populaire de Musique de Genève.*